The DRAGON Throne

The DRAGON Throne

Michael Cadnum

Viking

Viking

Published by Penguin Group

Penguin Young Readers Group, 345 Hudson Street, New York, New York 10014, U.S.A.

Penguin Group (Canada), 10 Alcorn Avenue, Toronto, Ontario, Canada M4V 3B2

(a division of Pearson Penguin Canada Inc.)

Penguin Books Ltd, 80 Strand, London WC2R 0RL, England

Penguin Ireland, 25 St Stephen's Green, Dublin 2, Ireland

(a division of Penguin Books Ltd)

Penguin Group (Australia), 250 Camberwell Road, Camberwell, Victoria 3124, Australia

(a division of Pearson Australia Group Pty Ltd)

Penguin Books India Pvt Ltd, 11 Community Centre, Panchsheel Park,

New Delhi - 110 017, India

Penguin Group (NZ), Cnr Airborne and Rosedale Roads, Albany, Auckland,

New Zealand (a division of Pearson New Zealand Ltd)

Penguin Books (South Africa) (Pty) Ltd, 24 Sturdee Avenue, Rosebank, Johannesburg 2196, South Africa

Penguin Books Ltd, Registered Offices: 80 Strand, London WC2R 0RL, England

Published in the U.S.A. by Viking, a division of Penguin Young Readers Group, 2005

1 3 5 7 9 10 8 6 4 2

LIBRARY OF CONGRESS CATALOGING-IN-PUBLICATION DATA IS AVAILABLE

ISBN: 0-670-03631-5

Printed in U.S.A.

Set in Granjon

Book design by Nancy Brennan

for Sherina

Day moon,
will you answer us
at last?

The
DRAGON
Throne

I

The Kingdom of the Lion

1

THE SKY OVER THE BROAD GREEN JOUSTING
field was blue, and the sun was bright.

Ester de Laci believed that it was a great shame that on
such a fine day a fighting man was likely to be killed in a
feat of arms. But all of London had turned out to see it—
including Prince John and his courtly guard—and so had
she.

The young lady stood on tiptoe, craning her neck within the crowd of other gentlefolk, a position from which it
was both proper and safe to observe bloodshed. Not yet, she
told herself.

Not yet.

She felt sick to her soul. She had never seen a joust
before, and for the moment she was not eager to have a very
good look at this one.

But at the same time she didn't want to miss it.

When Ester craned her neck and stood as tall as possible,
the young lady-in-waiting to Queen Eleanor could see
perfectly well as the master of the tournament let drop his

signal cloth. The rooks in the spring-bare trees around the field rose at the shock, the breathtaking crash of impact, two warhorses and two heavily armored men colliding under a clear sky.

The crowd cheered as a lance shattered, the shards spinning in the sunlight. Ester wanted to run away through the crowd to avoid the sight. How could a Christian city allow such a spectacle?

But she kept watching. The folk in the crowd called encouragement in London dialect to the young Englishman— *"Gif herm, Squire Hubert!"*

Hurt him, Hubert.

Hooves drummed once again across the grassy field, the brass fittings of the harnesses jingling in the collective intaken breath of the crowd.

The people around her gasped, a hundred throats silenced. The horses fought together, judging by the sounds of equine grunts—Ester had to look away again for an instant. "He's down!" cried an English voice, and another prayed aloud, "Hubert and Saint George!"

Saint George was a famous hero, the slayer of a dragon, and the patron saint of English fighting men. *Our Lady help them,* Ester preferred to pray, her eyes momentarily squeezed tight. And yet she felt the liveliest curiosity—the compelling urge to look and see what was happening.

The joust was a trial by combat, the just-returned Crusader squire Hubert of Bakewell battling Sir Nicholas de Foss. If Hubert succeeded, his fellow squire Edmund would go free and be considered innocent of the charges of theft recently leveled against him. If Nicholas triumphed, however, Edmund's life would be forfeit.

Edmund had looked every bit the stalwart and serious-minded young man, even bound by the bright royal chains. Ester did not know whether the charges against the tall, well-favored squire were true but like most of the gathered crowd, she cheered at the sight of him, and she prayed all the more fervently now that Heaven might spare his life.

Her father, the scholar Bernard de Laci, stood on his tiptoes and gave a cry of satisfaction. Ester tried to look, but the gentlefolk all around elbowed one another and blocked her view. She could clearly hear the sound of sword biting into shield. The weapon rang sharply against the edge of the opposing steel, even through the hubbub of curses and prayers. She would long remember the sound of a blow striking through surcoat and chain mail, into sinew or flesh, and the shudder of both satisfaction and compassion of the crowd all around her.

It had been a mistake to come here, she now believed. Only her duty as a daughter had convinced her to leave Westminster Castle and cross the river, and now here she was. She told herself that she would never by choice see another lance-and-sword contest as long as she lived. Ester turned to confide as much to Ida, her companion, but Ida had a cat's way of vanishing whenever unpleasantness was in the air.

She caught her father's arm and called into his ear,

nearly afraid to give voice to the question, "Father, what has happened?"

"Ester, praise Heaven," exclaimed Bernard. "Our English lad chopped the Frankish knight down like a stump!" He gave his daughter a sympathetic smile. "It's as well you did not see it, Ester," he added, "but it brought joy to this old bookman's heart."

"Our Lady be thanked," breathed Ester, grateful that Edmund could go free. She added a prayer for the soul of the vanquished Frankish man-at-arms.

But even then she could hear the Frankish squires drawing weapons, clashing them together to call attention, and swearing by Saint Michael that they would have revenge.

2

THESE ROUGH-CLAD SHIELD BEARERS HAD been drinking hard from goatskins of wine. All during the joust they had jostled each together and raised mailed fists, a dozen or so Chartrians with the crudest possible accents.

Ester could speak the language of Paris, and sing in a voice that her father said was like honey off a spoon. Despite her youth, she was a capable attendant to the royal mother of King Richard and Prince John. In earlier years Queen Eleanor had employed dozens of ladies of honor, but now kept only a few trusted companions of either great experience—or sterling promise.

Such ladies were usually of high or at least respected birth, and they were expected to be able to sew and soothe, remember the names of both knights and squires, and even, when the time came, to join their lady queen in hunting. Ester was convinced that knights were brutal sinners, and artless compared with the men and women of a royal court—although it had to be admitted that occasionally a fighting man was pleasing to look upon.

If I had a crossbow, Ester thought, I could teach these churls some manners.

This impulse did not surprise her. Ladies to the queen were expected to be gentle one moment, like iron the next. Bernard took Ester's arm protectively as the Frankish men-at-arms surged forward through the crowd of noblemen and pie sellers. A solidly built horse was pulled wide-eyed into the angry knot of Franks, and soon one man was mounted, crying *"sanc! sanc!"* demanding bloody revenge.

Another armed man pulled his wine-heavy frame into a saddle. Prince John's men drew around their royal English charge, halberds gleaming in the sunlight. The outnumbered Franks stirred, forced back by the greater number of the celebrants. Yet another steed was pressed into the melee, Frankish oaths and the flash of spurs working the snorting steeds through the crowd.

It was not unheard-of for a joust to end in a general melee, but Ester was surprised at such rude behavior in the presence of King Richard's brother, John. Even as she shrank with her father back through the shouting, excited crowd, she took heart at the glimpse she had of Sir Nigel of Nottingham climbing onto a mount himself and laying about him with a broadsword, punishing the angry Franks.

He was joined at once by the just-liberated Edmund Strongarm, who, having embraced Hubert and raised an open-faced salute to Heaven, now stirred to action. Without a helmet, and wearing only a surcoat over his wool sleeves, Edmund looked—in Ester's eyes—the very image of a Christian fighting man as he urged his mount between the ranks of drunken Frankish rioters and the royal person of Prince John.

One of the Frankish footmen brandished a halberd, a staff tipped with iron shaped into a point, a gleaming blade on either side of the shaft's tip. It was a staff designed to gouge out viscera or cut open the unprotected face.

Edmund seized this weapon as it thrust in his direction, grasping the long shaft with his two naked hands. It was no easy contest—the footman was built like a breed-boar, with a wide back and short legs. As Ester watched, Edmund wrested the weapon from his attacker, broke it in two, and flung the pieces away.

The square-jawed Jean de Chartres, tearful at the result of this joust, seized the bridle of Edmund's mount. The stocky older knight was convulsed with grief. He shook his gloved fist at Edmund.

"Frankish pigs," muttered a London voice nearby.

"Folk will believe that the blessed saints have decided the matter," her father confided to her, guiding her easily away from any further coarse language.

There was a certain good-spirited edge to his tone. It was a subject she and her father had discussed by candle-light. No churchman would have approved her father's skeptical view, that God's earth was replete with injuries and joys not authored by divine will.

Ester loved her father deeply, and respected his knowledge of both Greek and Latin. He had taught her to sign her name and read capably enough—few other women could tell *ego* from *egg*. But in secret she prayed that Heaven might forgive his inquiring soul. He had once confided that he did not believe that the queen's revered relics of Saint George were the bones of a saint at all, but simply the "knuckles of some man or woman no longer in need of them." Her father said most legendary saints were the stuff of candle smoke, little more than stories.

Bernard was tall and favored with aquiline features and eyes quick to show feeling, but he was not the sturdiest of men. It was her turn to force their way through the folk drawn toward the struggling band of fighting men, leading her father by the hand. The two of them were making slow progress. Already the force of arms and weight of disapproving people drove the Franks back, and farther back, horses kicking and slipping, growing so close that the heat from the anxious steeds swept over Ester.

She caught a glimpse of a red-faced spearman, his jaw set in effort as he fought to control his horse, all thought of revenge already lost as he struggled with the reins. The horse whinnied, the high, hysterical scream of a steed unused to such tumult.

Ester lost her father's hand in the sudden rush of stumbling men and women.

She cried out a warning.

Most reliable mounts had been shipped off with knights and squires to fight in the Crusade. This frightened animal, alarmed at the press of shouting people, tossed his head, broke the grip of his rider, and plunged forward.

Knocking Bernard to the ground.

The iron-shod hoof of the horse plunged into the fine-spun gown of the scholar's body, not once but twice.

Bernard gave out a shriek of pain.

3

THE HORSE WAS HAULED AWAY, SNORTING and wild-eyed.

The scholar writhed, unable to make a further sound.

Ester knelt beside her father, praying fervently under her breath to the Blessed Virgin, convinced against the evidence of her senses that her father was merely bruised, shaken, short of breath.

Ester had seen blood before. A gentlewoman was expected to know how to hunt, and she had seen hounds tearing the still-living deer, brought down by her own crossbow bolt. A person of good name was expected to be strong-hearted. Even her mild-tempered father enjoyed watching the mousing hawk return with its prey, and had bet a penny or two on the success of Ever-So, a favorite falcon of the queen's, which excelled at nabbing wood doves.

Bernard coughed, and his breath caught. His body twisted with an effort she felt in her own soul. His eyes found hers.

Still he could not speak.

The crowd fell silent, clearing a space, folk who did not

know the scholar by name or reputation recognizing in his dark gray mantle the garb of a prayerful man, a priest or man of letters.

Ida arrived from nowhere, a red-haired young woman with points of color in her cheeks. Judging by appearance, she could have been Ester's younger sister. "I've sent a boy for a doctor," said Ida. "And a priest," she added. Ida had a way of saying just that sole additional word one did not wish to hear.

The crowd parted silently, and for a moment the just-freed Edmund gazed down at Ester from horseback. He reassured his horse with one broad hand, the big, square-shouldered squire taking in the sight of the stricken scholar, his eyes quick with compassion.

"Don't move me," her father was saying when she put her ears close to his lips.

Or perhaps he was imploring "Please move me" as he coughed again and blood started at his nostrils and erupted from his mouth. The scholar reached up to take his daughter's hand as a voice sang out, "Way, make way," and Reginald de Athies, physician and astrologer, forced his way to Bernard's side and fell to his knees.

"You've taken hurt it seems, old friend," said the doctor.

Bernard spoke, but his voice was strengthless.

"No, we can't let you lie where you are," said the doctor. The physician looked to Ester. "We can't leave him here."

"Father, we have to move you," said Ester.

She could not hear him, but she understood his message: "It doesn't matter."

"The priest is on his way," Ida was saying, "that little Father Catald from Temple Church."

To give Bernard de Laci the final blessing, she was about to add, Ester was certain.

She held her father's hand and sensed his pulse—now strong, now ragged. She had kept a vigil not two years ago when her mother's lungs filled with water and she drifted into Heaven's company. Ester could not mistake the ever-weakening rhythm of her father's heartbeat, and she moved her lips in prayer.

Father Catald had a small man's way of slipping easily through a crowd, and he wore a fleece-white mantle marked with a large Templar cross that won him easy passage wherever he might go. Like any red-blooded Templar, he had been eager to see today's joust, Ester could imagine, and like any man of short stature, he had found a place well in front of the rest.

Before the pink-cheeked priest could begin any appropriate rite, Ester took his arm and insisted, "Bless me, Father."

"Quite willingly, Ester," said the blue-eyed priest in a tone of gentle wonderment.

"I am making a vow," Ester continued, "here and before Our Lady. If my father's life is spared, I swear before all Heaven to make a pilgrimage to Rome."

"Ester, this is more than a young lady should promise," responded the priest, looking more shaken by Ester's promise than by the sight of her stricken father. While not a warring man himself, the little man belonged to the famous fighting order of knights who carried swords in the name of God. He had been left behind by the other Templars so that he could hold daily mass in the nearly empty Temple Church.

Her father plucked at Ester's sleeve, his eyes wide with alarm. Vows were not undertaken lightly—a sacred promise could be no more easily dissolved than a marriage.

"Good Ester," Ida whispered, blinking her green eyes, "be careful what you swear."

"I vow it," Ester returned in her most fervent manner, "before Heaven's Queen."

4

EDMUND WAS RELUCTANT TO LEAVE THE place where the injured scholar lay, attended by a young woman in a well-made mantle and hood.

This fair young lady had hair the color of sunset at sea, a rare golden-red hue, and eyes the color of green a Crusader in the arid Holy Land could only dream of, the green of hillside and home.

Edmund would still be there in the dry, war-punished meadows near Acre and Jaffa, if an injury to Sir Nigel had not required them to voyage home. Edmund felt pity, even as he took in the sight of this comely young woman. It was a shame that an innocent onlooker had suffered an accident. He offered a prayer for the man's life.

A voice called his name. Edmund could not make quick progress through the churning crowd, and so many people made his horse nervous. He climbed down from his mount and remarked to Sir Rannulf, "There will be more trouble."

"They are only six wine-sick footmen," said Rannulf dismissively.

"And Sir Jean himself," added Edmund.

Sir Rannulf gave a gesture like a man swatting a flea—so much for Sir Jean.

Sir Rannulf of Josselin had slain five men in a legendary joust many years before, and, it was believed, killed countless Christians and Infidels since. His lips had been scarred by a would-be murderer's knife on one violent occasion, and Rannulf took care to shape his speech clearly as he responded, with what was, for the leathery knight, something of a chuckle. "Let us see them try their weapons."

Rannulf had nearly cut the throat of Nicholas as he lay mortally hurt just moments before, and only Hubert's intervention had preserved the young knight from Rannulf's sharp blade. Nonetheless, Nicholas was expected to expire within the hour. While Edmund judged himself no coward, it seemed to him that more men were killed under Heaven than necessity required.

A trumpet's notes rang out repeatedly, the brassy, all-alerting flurry slicing the murmur of voices, leaving only the sound of horses champing and shaking their bridles.

A voice was lifted yet again. "Edmund Strongarm and Hubert of Bakewell," sang out this fine voice, in the tones of a herald. "The squires Edmund and Hubert—attend you now to the prince."

King Richard had proven an impetuous, energetic leader of men during the Crusade; his brother, Prince John, was reckoned untrustworthy by King Richard's cohorts. The prince had promised to stay away from England while Richard was crusading, and the war in the Holy Land was far from finished. Edmund could not fathom the nature of this princely command.

The herald was calling again, his bright eyes and clean-shaven face looking in Edmund's direction.

It was the nature of heralds to deliver tidings and requests in a formal, slightly obscure manner. Anxiety pricked Edmund, and he wondered how difficult it would be to flee across the field of trampled daffodils.

"What does this mean?" Edmund asked.

"What else can it mean?" answered Rannulf. "Except that Prince John means some mischief. He is a grasping man, with love for no one."

"Am I," asked Edmund, "to be put in chains again?"

The thought took the breath from his body. Edmund rubbed the chafed places where until scant minutes before manacles had kept him under the law's command. The previous night's imprisonment had seemed endless. Although it was not the first time Edmund had seen prison rats and smelled the dank, fetid matting of prison bedding straw, he prayed he would never spend another such night.

"We are all in chains," said Rannulf, with what for this scarred warrior was a smile. "Of one sort or another."

"Straighten your tunic," Sir Nigel was saying, hurrying around Edmund and adjusting his clothing.

Rannulf performed the same office for Hubert, straightening the squire's surcoat and brushing blades of grass from his sleeve. Hubert's gaze was solemn, the young squire's conscience just beginning to absorb the act of legal homicide he had committed moments before.

"Keep your eyes downcast," advised Nigel.

It was considered ill-mannered in the extreme to look into the gaze of a royal prince. Kings, queens, and princes were rulers blessed by God. No ordinary mortal approached such a person except with a feeling of awe—and anxiety.

"Prince John," said Nigel in a tone of pride and concern, "wants to have a closer look at you."

5

PRINCE JOHN WAS STANDING UNDER A
canopy, a gleaming yellow jewel on his finger. The stone was
topaz, Edmund recognized, on a well-worked silver ring.
The younger brother of King Richard sported a short, well-
tended beard, and when he smiled, his teeth were white.

Edmund knelt beside Hubert, the two squires like
young men at prayer, the taller, brown-haired Edmund
taking as his cue the behavior of his better-educated, fair-
haired friend.

The heartbeat was swift in his chest. Edmund had
dreamed of such a moment, it was true. He had eased into
sleep, and stirred to full wakefulness with fantasies of a
moment of recognition before a royal lord, but he had
known even as a boy that such events never really happen.
The toil of the war, and the slaughter of some two thousand
innocent prisoners at King Richard's command, had taught
him that crowned kings and battle glory were sweeter in
song than in life.

"Sir Rannulf of Josselin," the prince was saying, "it
would please me to borrow your sword."

"My lord prince," said Rannulf, presenting his sword, the blade across his two upraised palms. "It does me honor," added the veteran killer of men, and Edmund noted how the words of high speech turned Rannulf from a weathered manslayer to the semblance of a *gentil* knight.

"I would make the two of you, young Edmund and young Hubert, into knights," said Prince John with the barest smile.

The singing of Edmund's own heart, the buzz of sounds and voices, memories and hopes, made the next words sound far away.

"But first you must pledge to me your loyalty and honor," said the prince. "Above any other man."

While any knight had the power to welcome a squire into knighthood, to have a prince perform the honor was a rare privilege.

But Edmund gave a glance toward Hubert, took in the sight of his friend's troubled gaze, and spoke for both of them. "My lord prince, we are in England on behalf of King Richard and Sir Maurice, his representative in Rome."

"Good Sir Maurice de Gray, such an honorable man," said Prince John smoothly. "And his daughter, Galena, is a beauty, by every account."

"We owe our loyalty to Richard, your brother, by God's grace our king," said Edmund, feeling the strength leave his voice. No squire had ever spoken to a royal prince so boldly, Edmund was certain.

"Do you indeed?" said Prince John. "Are you my brother's creatures?"

"So we are, if our lord prince might well forgive us," said Hubert in agreement.

Edmund was glad to hear his friend speak up—Hubert had always been the better phrase smith.

"I think I will not forgive you," said Prince John. "I had this day wagered a purse of new silver against bold Hubert here. And lost every ounce."

"My lord prince," said Hubert, sounding politely woeful, "may it return to you tenfold."

"You two can repay this silver," said the prince, "by entering my service as knights."

"Alas, my lord prince," Sir Nigel said. "Their honor will not permit it."

"You displease me," said the prince after a long pause, during which no one dared to speak. "All of you."

"And yet, my lord prince," said Nigel, steel in his voice, "you could still name these two squires worthy knights, if Heaven gives you the grace."

"Sir Nigel," said the prince, "I have no reason to weigh your opinion with any favor."

"I am but a sinner, and a killer of men," said Sir Rannulf, speaking carefully and formally through his scarred lips. "Even so I am a Christian, my lord prince, and on my honor I commend these squires to you."

The prince chewed on the knuckle of his thumb. For a long moment he did not speak, and glared at the four fighting men as though he now wished that the earth would open and swallow them.

At last the prince gave a shrug. "Because your manslaughter is so renowned, Rannulf, I will do as you suggest."

It took only a few heartbeats.

The prince stood. He touched Hubert's shoulders with the blade, and said something too thrilling to be easily understood by Edmund's dazzled senses. Then it was Edmund's own turn.

The voice of the king's younger brother continued as though from far across the kingdom, adding, "In the name of Our Lady, Saint Michael, and Saint George."

A great cheer erupted as the prince added the words, "Edmund, be thou a knight."

Edmund believed it all the more when he glimpsed Hubert's smile of amazement.

Elviva will be amazed, thought Edmund. I was too lowly in the past, a mere moneyer's apprentice, to suggest marriage.

He could imagine the delight in her eyes.

"You'll feast with me tonight," Prince John was heard to say. "Sir Edmund and Sir Hubert—I am not finished with you."

The prince smiled, too, but his countenance showed anger more than joy.

Edmund felt a hand grasp his arm at the wrist, a firm grip that got his attention despite the crowd of well-wishers all around. It was the Templar priest who had been at the side of the injured scholar, a short man with bright eyes and the Templar cross that Edmund had learned to respect during the Crusade.

The cleric stood as tall as he could to murmur, "Come to Temple Church for prayers before sunset."

"With pleasure, Father," said Edmund, bending low to take in a further message.

"And tell no one," added the priest. "If you ever wish to see Rome again."

6

ESTER TOOK HOPE FROM THE FACT THAT her father had stopped coughing, but it was a shaky courage, strongly braced by prayer.

The river all around was rising, and this alone was enough to trouble her. Bernard opened his eyes every few moments, finding his daughter with his gaze and giving her a weak smile. She held his hand, keeping hold of it even when the tide of the Thames tossed the boat.

The doctor, Reginald de Athies, advised the boatmen to row with more measured strokes. "Like a maid churning butter."

"I am greatly sorry my lords and my lady," said the taller boatman, a fresh-faced youth outfitted in the shapeless gray cap and smock of his trade.

River water sloshed over the side, and Bernard shifted weakly, the wet mixing with the blood on his gown, diluting it.

"Good lad, you are getting river on my patient," said the doctor.

"The current, sire," said the young boatman, "is no respecter of suffering."

"What a tongue twitches in the mouth of this knave," said the doctor, as though pleased to have an object for his growing impatience. "Who taught you to speak to your superiors in such a tone, boat keeper?"

"A gentleman passing over the river to the joust," said the boatman, with an airy calm, "was just as learned as any on the river now, and this fine charitable knight gave us both a quarter penny."

"Silver you've spent on ale," said the physician with growing heat.

"A knight from some distant place, where coin is the only language," the boatman continued, rowing with energy.

England was slowly seeing evidence of foreign adventurers, older knights and younger vagabonds. With most fighting folk of honor on Crusade with King Richard, and only now beginning to return from the Holy Land, many foreign men-at-arms had attached themselves to Prince John's cause, and found much work in collecting taxes and enforcing laws. Some wandering knights were rumored to be at large in the woods, extorting money and chattel from peasants and yeoman farmers.

"We bought the dearest Rhenish wine," the boatman was recounting, rowing all the harder against the current. "We enjoyed wonderful huge pitchers of it, until we could not swallow more."

Reginald gave Ester a pat of reassurance, as if to say "I'll deal with this impertinent rower." It was just a quick touch on the bare skin of her forearm, but that slight contact was enough to cause Ester to grow impatient herself.

"There is no need to chide the boatmen, good doctor," she said.

"When churls drink costly foreign wine," replied the doctor, "the world's turned upside down."

It seemed to Ester that the distant bank would never arrive, and that it approached only to shrink back again, unattainable reeds and mossy pebbles.

Westminster Castle was some distance west of London's walls, not far from the river in a countryside of oaks and hedgerows. The castle was handsome, in the way of buildings constructed to endure siege and gradually transformed to a place of royal shelter. Arrow slits marked the high walls, narrow openings where crossbowmen could aim their weapons, and guards leaned against their spears in the manner of a drawing a child might make, towers and battlements, every soul with a cheerful duty.

Sheep and cattle grazed across the flowery field, and somewhere a tool was being repaired, the sweet sound of hammer on scythe. In the distance a farmer's wife shoveled ashy lime, engaged in making soap. The boat nosed the close-shorn grasses of the riverbank, and Bernard gave an involuntary wince, and then smiled in apology. A strong-hearted scholar, he had always taught Ester, should never complain.

The injured man was met by men supporting a litter-bed. Ida, who had traveled ahead to fetch these attendants, beckoned them to hurry. The horsemen wore the livery of the royal Plantagenets, a leopard in red on the chest of every tunic. Only a careful eye could discern the worn hems of some of the garments, and the occasional faintly starlike design where a moth hole had been repaired by stitchery.

If there was a single fact about court life Ester did not admire, it was the careful protocol that dictated every act a castle servant might commit. Ester had seen country folk, shepherds and haywards running on market day, bounding stride by stride toward home, or sprinting merrily toward a beckoning friend, but the men and women of the royal court never hurried. To break into a run was thought ungentle—no lady would think of skipping down a corridor, or rushing after a herald with further instructions.

Even now, with her father's life in the balance, the liveried servants took measured steps as they found their way down the bank of the river and listened to the doctor's instructions on how to lift his stricken patient.

"It will be like the time the churchmen moved the relics of Saint Gwen," said the doctor, referring to the recent reburial and celebration of the skeleton of a local holy woman. The pious had gathered from far away to see the centuries-old bones swaddled in sendal, a rare silk, and buried with sung devotions.

"Gently, gently," the doctor called now, as the scholar offered a brave smile and let his body be lifted slowly— more slowly than the monks lifting the amber-and-walnut remains of the blessed Gwen.

"Wait," her father called in a whisper, squeezing his

daughter's hand in anticipation of the pain soon to follow as they were about to lower him onto the litter-bed.

Giffard, a white-haired knight and steward to the queen, murmured to the scholar, "We will do you no harm, my lord Bernard."

Ester was grateful for the measured, time-consuming deliberateness of the servants as they eased Bernard onto the portable bed frame with such care that only once did Bernard give a start of pain.

Was it Ester's imagination? Or did she actually hear one servant murmur in a shaken voice to another, "He'll be dead by dawn"?

7

WHEN HE WAS SECURE ON THE LITTER-BED,
Bernard raised his head to look around, thanking the servants as they lifted their load to their shoulders, much as
pallbearers carry a loved one to the churchyard.

"There's no need," the scholar mouthed, "for all this
trouble."

"They'll see you safely home, Bernard," said the doctor,
with an air of professional cheer, "where you can drink hot
wine and rest your head on a downy pillow."

"And be pitching quoits by summer," said his daughter
reassuringly.

A leisurely game of throwing the disc-shaped stone
toward a target was one of her father's favorite pastimes,
and he and his daughter sported often, long into the slow-
fading evenings of June. Ester fixed the image of a twilight
match between them, the smooth stone clanging against the
iron post.

To her displeasure, the doctor took the sleeve of her
gown as the litter was born quickly and yet with care
toward the castle gate.

"Ester," said the doctor, speaking in a soft voice, "if you will permit me, I should detail the nature of your father's injuries."

"My father will play half-bowl with you, good doctor, on Midsummer's Eve."

"I have every prayer that it might be so," said the doctor. "And yet, dear Ester, I have gazed upon—" He hesitated, but having begun, took a breath and continued. "I have studied dead felons hanging, as the law decrees, and seen, if you will forgive me for mentioning it, their bones as flesh retires."

Ester had noticed that men sometimes went out of their way to display talents that made them tedious. She kept her voice the very example of patience. "My father needs me at his bedside, Doctor."

Reginald de Athies was a round-faced man with gray eyes. Ester knew he was unmarried. He was taking more pains than he would for a matron or a merchant, eager to impress Ester with his medical lore and windy diction.

"The ribs are exposed as weather and winged creatures have their way," the doctor was saying, "as you may have observed yourself."

"If you will let me join my father," was all Ester would allow herself to say, in no frame of mind to discuss decaying criminals.

"The ribs of a body form something like a wicker frame," continued Reginald, "or bushel basket, containing our lights and other organs."

Ester was walking, as quickly as she could without

breaking into a run, but the doctor was keeping the pace. "And I fear," he added, "that the hoof broke your father's ribs."

Scrolls of precious sheepskin brooded on shelves, waiting for the touch of Bernard de Laci's quill. A priceless volume, Marcus Aureliuss' *Meditations*, was open on the lectern in the corner, the dark letters distinct against the surface of the vellum.

The late King Henry, father to Richard and John, had endowed Bernard's studies, saying that the wise man was an ornament to his court. The de Laci family had an estate near the Seine at Honfleur, and land near the village of Beer along the English coast, but they had never been wealthy enough to thrive except by serving the crown. Bernard had confided to Ester that the old king would rather hear of Caesar's military victories in Gaul than the Nature of Virtue, and that the new king, Richard, had little use for either. In contrast, the legendary Eleanor of Aquitaine had enjoyed the consolations of philosophy during the long winter nights away from her sons, and often asked the scholar to read to her.

In recent weeks the queen had kept to her own chamber, plagued, some said, by illness. Ester knew that the queen drew strength from solitude, an unusual trait. Constant companionship, song and chatter, filled the days of rich and poor.

It was rumored that Queen Eleanor had followed John's journey here to make certain that he did not cause too much mischief in Richard's kingdom. In a world in which the eldest son inherited most of the wealth and power, younger sons were often lean and restless, and Ester reckoned John as hungry as any man alive.

"Ruth?" her father called weakly from his bed.

It was the name of Ester's mother, dead these long seasons ago.

If Bernard was surprised to see his daughter sitting beside him, and not his wife, he gave no sign. He reassured Ester, silently forming the words, "Don't fear for me."

Some people said the right combination of syllables could catch the Devil's attention. Sometimes Ester was frightened at the way words in the open books of ancient learning seemed to dance and shift in candlelight. Her father was a wise man, and had explained to his daughter the dignified life of a Stoic, but now Ester wondered if too many hours with a pagan philosopher might have put his soul in jeopardy.

By any purely rational measure, Ester realized, her father was close to death.

Before nightfall it began to rain outside, the soft music of falling drops against the wooden window shutters. Reginald searched his patient's chest with his fingers, pressing gently. Her father gave a moan without waking, and Reginald met Ester's eyes.

"The damage may be great," he said. "As I had feared."

He sat with Ester long into the night, as the candles burned down and began to gutter. Ida set out a new candle, a long white taper, as Bernard sank from a restless half-awakened state to an uneasy slumber, and at last into a deep torpor, sweat beading on his brow.

Ester silently renewed her vow to go on a pilgrimage to Rome. But it was enough to challenge her faith, the way her father's breath slowed down so completely. He held it and kept it shut within his lungs to the count of twenty of her own heartbeats before he exhaled again—a long, phlegm-choked sigh.

Besides, her vow, while solemn, had been rash. She had neither gold nor rich jewels. While it was true she dressed herself with care, she had stitched her gown herself, with her own silver thimble and thread.

No one in the queen's court had a robust purse. A pilgrimage to Rome was a costly undertaking, requiring horses and armed protectors. Such a journey was beyond her means, and beyond her hopes.

As though to remind her of this, Heaven seemed to chide Ester for her idle promise. Her father lifted a hand to point out something only he could see, some vision in his fever dream.

His hand faltered.

And fell back.

8

AT SOME HOUR WELL INTO THE NIGHT, Reginald felt for the pulse of his patient, made the sign of the cross as he muttered a prayer, and said, "I'll be here when day breaks." He hesitated, and added, "Ester, you should seek rest yourself."

She used a soft linen to gently bathe her father's face and hands. Our Lady's watchfulness upon the living never ends, Ester knew.

But she felt some sympathy for the doctor, well-meaning for all his pride. "Perhaps your star charts will foretell some joy for you," she offered, troubled by the shadows under the doctor's eyes.

"Only one hope would bring me joy," the doctor responded, once again touching her hand with his. "Aside from the sound of Bernard's laughter again, as he betters me at chess."

When they were alone with the sick man, Ida brought Ester a lamb's-wool shawl against the chill of the spring night.

Ida de Mie was a year younger than Ester, and likewise unwed. She had stitchwork beside her, an embroidered griffin, pale gray wool against a green field. The fabric was reworked remnants from a minstrel's tunic, the beefy Rahere le Grand, who had died at table on Saint Stephen's Day, facedown in his soup. Ida and Ester had refashioned the fine wool, fixing it so that no eye could detect the old thread-holes or the way the fabric was gently faded. Ida and Ester were equally skilled at needlework, and knew the feather and the chain stitch as well as they knew the stories of the Our Lady's miracles.

Ida's parents had both drowned when an ancient footbridge across the River Exe had collapsed during the feast of Saint Agatha three winters before. This personal loss had encouraged in Ida a tendency to offer trenchant opinions, none the easier to bear because they were usually accurate.

"The doctor chews cinnamon bark," asserted Ida in her usual quiet monotone, "to sweeten his breath."

"I have never noticed," Ester heard herself say.

"You pay him too little heed, Ester, or I'm a mouse."

Ida's good family name made her Ester's social equal, but she generally adopted the role of Ester's shadow, both assistant and adviser on matters of dress or conduct. Swept by inner turmoil, Ester could not suppress the thought that, in truth, Ida did resemble some small, intense rodent. As Ester parted her lips to urge her friend to find some sleep, Ida hushed her with a raised finger.

Ida cocked her head. *Listen!*

Then her eyes grew round, and she whispered, "She's coming!"

A page stepped into the room, a youth dressed in a flowing yellow tabard—a well-woven overgarment—and carrying a silver candleholder. Shadows danced across his features as he gave the two young ladies a sympathetic glance.

Ester's heart beat fast. There was no time to get ready!

There was an artful protocol to such moments. Furniture had to be squared against the wall, excess wax pinched from candles, the chamber pot hidden behind curtains. Ester had barely time to make these improvements and smooth her father's bedding, with Ida's help. She shook out the folds of her gown to straighten them, and then, with no further warning, a shadow fell across the room.

Ester and Ida knelt.

With a rustle of garments and the gentle kissing sound of leather slippers on the stone floor, a figure scented with rose water swept into the room. This personage remained unmoving as she observed her two youthful ladies-in-waiting and, Ester sensed, took in the uneven whisper of Bernard's breathing.

"Ester, arise," said a woman's voice, perhaps inadvertently ignoring Ida.

Ester did as she was told, and stood in the candlelit presence of Queen Eleanor, mother to King Richard and Prince John.

The gray-haired queen was clad in a long-sleeved

cote—a sweeping, flowing garment—dyed in rare vermil-ion. A few minutes of bright sun would begin to fade such a rich color, and it was possible to observe, even by candle-light, the margins of the sleeves, where usage and light had done some harm.

The queen stepped to the bedside of the dying man.

Ester was too overcome with feeling to make a sound.

"God's teeth," said the queen, her voice taut with emotion.

Ester made the sign of the holy cross.

The queen continued, "I'd gut the horse that did this with my own hand."

Eleanor of Aquitaine had journeyed on Crusade some fifty years earlier, beside her first husband, Louis, the king of France. She had headed a throng of one hundred of her ladies-in-waiting. The pope of those days, Eugenius III, had been furious, and had forbidden women on Crusade ever since, even though he had at one time admired the young Eleanor, and had given her a special token of divine favor.

The queen kept this holy relic in a silver reliquary, locked and out of sight. It was an object too wonderful for ordinary daylight.

Queen Eleanor spoke to the comatose scholar in a voice heavy with sorrow. "I fear you will not survive this, good Bernard."

"My lady queen," Ester heard herself interject, "I trust he will."

"How, dear Ester?" prompted the queen.

The mother of King Richard spoke a blend of fighting-man's Frankish and courtly high speech. Ester had never known Queen Eleanor to speak English. In old age she had the beauty of wood or polished stone, her eyes the color of sun on fertile soil, brown laced with gold. Her glance, as the songs told, quickened the hearts of heroes, and silenced fools.

Ester was startled at herself for daring to exchange opinions with the queen. A young woman of Ester's station was intended to listen carefully and make of conversation a sort of chanson—an artful song, filled with references to wild roses and the courtship of swans.

Perhaps, then, there was a touch of hard metal to the queen's voice when she insisted, "Ester, what can we do to save the life of my old friend?"

9

SIR EDMUND.

Edmund rolled the name again in his mouth.

His new condition made his arms and legs feel foreign. He felt newly assembled, like a figure of dough rolled out by a baker, ready for the oven. He savored the daydream of telling Elviva how he had knelt and heard the prince mint a new knight as certainly as a hammer turns a bit of silver into a coin.

"Do not permit yourselves to go to Prince John's feast tonight," Father Catald was saying, pouring them each a cup of spiced wine.

"We were invited to a banquet," retorted Hubert, "along with Sir Nigel and Sir Rannulf, and we would show no disrespect to the king's brother." He added, a little wistfully, "I would so much enjoy a feast."

Father Catald raised his eyebrows and put a finger to his lips.

Heavy steps plodded past in the rain, accompanied by the *rap-rap-rap* of a spear carried like a walking staff. The watchman's voice lifted in a singsong, "Well and all well," ready for a long night of duty.

Edmund sipped wine and considered his fortunes. The two freshly minted knights had celebrated holy mass in the circular sanctuary of Temple Church. It was fitting and traditional for new knights to offer thanksgiving to Heaven, and Edmund's prayers had been heartfelt.

Sir Nigel had found the church with little trouble, but could not participate in devotions, being drunk. He slept now like an effigy in the shadowy confines of the church, watched over by his friend Rannulf.

Their prayers complete, the two new knights sat in the priest's chambers, just across the courtyard from the church. It was dark outside. No one in London could guess their whereabouts, Edmund reckoned. They had donned travelers' hooded mantles and taken separate, roundabout routes, at Catald's bidding, through the byways of London, before arriving at the sanctuary. Now a gentle rain murmured across the sandstone windowsill.

The priest slipped to the window, and listened. Then he shut each iron-framed wooden shutter, and fastened it with a latch. "Every wood pigeon is a spy for the prince," he explained with a relieved smile. "And every rat a cutthroat."

Edmund kept quiet, trying to judge Catald's character.

It was true that he liked the pink-cheeked little priest, and enjoyed his London English, laced with Latin and Norman Frankish. But Edmund had been unlucky—or unwise—in his judgment of both master and servant in recent years. He had served as apprentice to a good-hearted counterfeiter in Nottingham, and on the voyage home found himself unwitting master to a talented thief. He admitted to himself that he no longer had any trust in his ability to assess men and determine their motives.

"Please realize, Father Catald," Hubert was saying, indicating the earth-brown bread and flinty cheese before them on the table, "we are all very hungry." This was simple—even monkish—fare, although the wine, flavored with cardamom and colored with turnsole blossoms, was warming to the soul. "It's been many long months," added Hubert, "since Edmund here enjoyed anything like real food."

"You both would relish the prince's farced pheasant, that much is beyond question," said Father Catald, pouring them each more mulled wine, "and such savories as new-born piglets. And you'd welcome further servings of the excellent venison he poaches from his brother's forests."

"It's true, then," said Hubert thoughtfully, "that Prince John usurps Richard's properties."

"Much as the stoat," said the little cleric, "unsettles the rabbit hutch."

Edmund spoke at last. "Forgive me a blunt question, Father, but why should we trust your judgment?" It was hard to frame such a query to a man of God, and Edmund offered a smile of apology.

But at the same time he kept his gaze steady.

"As Master of the Temple I am chosen by my fellow Templars," said Catald, "and these men would not name a fool to maintain such a holy place. Besides, I serve here with the personal blessing of the king." The Templars were a religious order of fighters who took vows of chastity and devotion to Heaven. Their efforts in the Holy Land had included providing nourishment for King Richard's Crusaders, and Edmund could recall no shameful act ever committed by a Templar.

"You are loyal to Richard," offered Edmund.

"As you must be," said Father Catald, "second, of course, to your loyalty to God. At the same time, I am aware that neither of Queen Eleanor's sons are likely candidates for sainthood."

"We must return to Rome," Edmund said. "We owe it to King Richard and his envoy there."

"I pledged my word," said Hubert, "to the Lady Galena."

Galena and her father Sir Maurice relied on Hubert and his friends to return to strife-torn Rome with news regarding the state of London politics. Furthermore, Hubert had personal, emotional ties to Galena that required his journeying back by any means.

The priest gave a nod of understanding, but said nothing further.

"Why should we offend the prince," asked Hubert, "even if we do fail to trust him?"

"Tonight," responded Father Catald, "unless I mistake

the prince badly, he will seek your vows of fealty." *Of feaute.* "You will become Prince John's creatures, or he will make you suffer."

A promise of fealty, Edmund knew, made a man the vassal of his lord. A lord's *creature* was even further indebted, although such men were often made wealthy. Edmund and Hubert had already seen the power of court intrigue on their companion from Italy, Luke de Warrene. That smooth-talking knight had been sent by Sir Maurice, distinguished banneret and Richard Lionheart's envoy in Rome, to discover how matters stood in London. Sir Luke had vanished into the corridors of the city, bought off, Nigel had suggested, by Prince John.

"Surely Prince John will cause us no injury," said Edmund, with a weak laugh.

"He will roast you over hardwood coals," said the priest. "Especially you, Sir Edmund. The prince no doubt believes that old rumor—that you know the location of some hidden silver."

"My former master was a kind but dishonest man," said Edmund, sorrow in his voice. "And he paid for his crimes with his life. I know of no hidden treasure."

"Besides, our worthy prince is jealous," said the priest. "Men love Richard for his courage—and dislike John for his avarice."

"We can flee London," said Hubert, in the bright way he might have said, "We can buy a goat."

Edmund gave his friend a patient glance. "Your father

is a wool merchant, with a pantry crowded with servants."

"A few," admitted Hubert.

"I have no more silver than a scarecrow." Even his war hammer, Edmund reflected, had been lost in a shipwreck off the shore of Italy.

"We could make our way home," said Hubert. "My father would be glad to see every one of us—although one look at Rannulf would make him uneasy. Unless some murrain has stricken the sheepfolds, he can afford to send us to Rome and pay for Edmund's armor at the same time."

Knighthood had already given Hubert a new manner. He had always been quick with a smile, and just as quick with a sword. Now Hubert was demonstrating that he was a man of formidable plans, and the means to carry them out.

And Hubert's suggestion ignited Edmund's hopes. The insistent dream of seeing Elviva again, the young woman with whom he'd shared hopes for a future, had been too long nurtured in his heart. And Maud, his master's widow—he'd be able to see both of them, and show them that he'd survived battle, and thrived.

And the winding, homely streets of Nottingham—he'd be able to walk the muddy lanes and see the tavern louts and the street-pigs. He wanted to go home.

"You'd ride with manhunters trailing you every step of the way," cautioned the priest.

Hubert leaned forward, and continued intently, "Please find Edmund a sword—or a war hammer, if it is in your power."

"And you'll need mounts, and enough coin to pay for your bread and ale," said the priest with an air of mock-exasperation.

"Yes," agreed Hubert, "we'll need all of that."

Father Catald's words were solemn but his eyes merry as he added, "Do I look like a man of miracles?"

10

THE EARLY MORNING WAS COLD.

The four knights rode north. The road was bright with the previous night's rain. A holy man leaned on his staff and raised a shaky gesture of blessing. Such wandering souls were poor and sometimes so devout that they spoke only to pray.

Edmund searched in the new leather purse and selected a silver penny, stamped with the likeness of old King Henry—Father Catald had been generous. Edmund asked, the holy man, "Have any men-at-arms passed this way?"

"None but you, blessed Crusaders," came the trembling response. The holy traveler was gaunt, and clung to his staff with a red-knuckled fist. A silver penny was more money than most poor folk saw in months, and he gazed at the coin in disbelief as his fingers closed around it.

A determined three-day ride could bring them to Nottingham, some one hundred English miles away, if rivers had not overflowed their banks and outlaws did not attack them. Rannulf held back at times, listening, and sometimes circling far off so that his three companions lost sight of him. Relief overcame Edmund each time Rannulf's mount cantered back into view.

Nigel insisted that he had no headache, none at all, and that no man in the kingdom felt better than he. He stopped twice to empty his belly, however, vomiting hard without leaving the saddle, and at last conceded that in his travels to the Holy Land he had grown unused to English wine.

Given the parlous state of horse trading in London, they were all reasonably well mounted. Father Catald had said that between the horse levies taking worthy mounts on Crusade, and the greed of Prince John, every animal at the weekly Smooth Field market was likely to be "in an evil condition." But the Templar religious order was far from impoverished and stabled the best horses the town could offer.

Edmund rode a *lyard*—spotted gray—horse, a stocky, spirited steed. Hubert rode a dun-colored mount of similar character. Edmund privately christened his horse Surefoot, hoping that the name might work some magic.

The two older knights urged on two charcoal-dark steeds that had appeared serviceable in the early dawn light of the Templar stables. The tails of both dark beasts had been docked—cut short. Edmund wondered if this harsh practice had soured the creatures toward men in general. Rannulf had by far the most quarrelsome animal, the horse complaining through its bit, and tossing its rein chains, the fine Templar equipment chiming noisily.

"He's a scold, this one," was all Rannulf would say. For

all his harsh appearance, he was steady with his mount, even gentle, and made soft hushing sounds through his scarred lips.

Peasants straightened from their work at the approach of the four knights. That they were Crusaders home from abroad could be determined by the fading crosses displayed on their surcoats, and any hope that they might pass unremarked grew faint in Edmund's heart as farmers and goose maids waved and called out, "God speed you home!"

As forest closed around them, Edmund put a hand to his new sword. Of every act of generosity and advice Father Catald had offered, this was, in Edmund's view, the most thrilling. The sword was one of many that had belonged to the legendary Raymund of Chalk, a knight who had once fought the renowned Baldwin of Bec and had been briefly taken hostage, only to escape when Baldwin's squire slipped and fell into a ditch full of brewing lees.

What made the weapon all the more remarkable was that within its pommel, well secured beneath an inset of rock crystal, was a dark fleck of bone—the relic of a saint.

Rannulf approached again, and his charger pranced and complained as the bearded knights reined to a stop.

"Five men riding, after us," he said, "in the prince's livery and not sure of the route."

"Are they lost?" asked Hubert hopefully.

"Not lost," said Rannulf, with a dry laugh, "and they can just about tell our tracks from the general muck along the road." The knight drew the blade from his scabbard and examined its edge in the late morning sun. He cut at a mote in the shaft of sunlight, the heavy weapon making a low-toned whisper.

"Rannulf, your horse has worms," said Nigel. He was leaning from the saddle, examining the dung just now deposited by Rannulf's animal.

"Worms or not," said Rannulf, "I've already taught him to be a fighting man's mount."

"Every animal you ever rode was ruled by fear, Rannulf," teased Nigel. "I handle my mounts with a loving touch, as I handle a woman."

"I wager a full penny," said Rannulf, "that I could ride even a worm-shot hackney through the trackless wood, and out the other side, leaving you in the mud."

Nigel laughed. Although he had been injured in the Battle of Arsuf—so badly that he had been forced to retire from the Holy Land, and might never regain perfect strength—no knight, Edmund thought, had a more resilient spirit.

"Take the wager or not," said Rannulf.

Edmund realized that the two older knights were giving themselves a joking rationale for parting company with their younger companions. But it was a pleasing fiction, this mock challenge, and it would give the prince's men a trail to confuse them, wending off into the oak-wood hunting reserve.

Besides, even now Rannulf's horse was lifting his nose and giving out an equine equivalent of "Why are we waiting?" Soon the prince's men would be able to hunt them by sound alone.

Nigel took the bridle of Edmund's horse in his gloved hand. "We'll meet in Nottingham."

Before Edmund could protest, the two older knights worked their horses over cart-ruts of the road, and into the twilight of the surrounding forest.

Edmund and Hubert rode on for a while. "We'll meet in Nottingham," said Hubert, sounding very much like the drink-punished Nigel.

Edmund gave a laugh, but it sounded mirthless in his own ears.

The shadows shifted and shrank. Some evil-sounding bird—or phantom—chuckled overhead. "I had forgotten how unholy an English forest can be," breathed Hubert.

Edmund put his hand once more on the pommel of the sword. This relic, a mere freckle of bone, was a blessed remnant of Saint Breoc, a divine noted for his acts of charity. Putting his hand on the weapon's hilt made Edmund feel closer to Heaven.

"I've heard," said Edmund, with an affected carelessness, "that every tree hides a devil."

"A ghost," amended Hubert.

"The headless wraith of a murdered woman," asserted Edmund, not to be outdone, "lurks behind every hornbeam bush."

Edmund and Elviva had sat near the fire talking about

the high fairies who lived in such woods. It seemed so long ago to Edmund now. No Christian alive enjoyed a wilderness setting, whether wood or scrubland, beach or windy moor. Any such place was wasteland, in the view of most folk. Although a peat-cutter or an outlaw might have some grudging appreciation of a wild scene for practical reasons, no one in Edmund's experience had ever looked upon a forest with love.

Edmund's father had been a cooper—a freedman who had lived by cutting oak into barrel staves. The family had dwelled in a thatched cottage at the edge of Sherwood Forest, and Edmund recalled legends of a naked man with antlers like a stag who lived near the Knaresborough cliffs.

A further birdcall echoed, and a branch somewhere crashed in the shadowy vaults of the place, a resounding presence that spread a baffled, half-lost murmur that faded into silence.

"Heaven be my shield," said Hubert fervently. "I would not travel alone through this forest for my weight in silk."

Edmund was about to add his hearty agreement, but the sound of approaching horsemen from behind spurred them to ride faster.

Their saddles were gently curved riding saddles, not the heavy war or jousting furnishings. And the horses responded to their riders, taking sport in what for them must have been a willing race against the horses far behind, giving way to a rocking rhythm they could continue for a long time without fatigue.

But whenever Edmund and Hubert paused to let their chargers rest or nuzzle the shadow-clawed waters of a stream, the sound of pursuit was ever closer, along with the voices of men urging their mounts.

At last Edmund seized Hubert's arm as they splashed through a stream spilling across the road.

The riders following them were many more than Edmund had expected. Judging by the noise they made, they were a gathering force, chain mail jingling as they came on.

Hubert gave a gesture, *Follow me.*

The two entered the tangled woodland. A pair of wings darted off in alarm. A branch caught at Edmund's sleeve, and his horse half-stumbled on a bristling, moss-shaggy log.

It seemed to Edmund that at once they were lost.

11

BUT THEY MADE GOOD PROGRESS, DOWN deer trails and through streams, disturbing the broad, gleaming leaves of bracken-fern. Wood-gathering women directed them northward, charcoal burners and fowlers encouraging them with ever more northern-sounding accents. "It's only two day's ride now, my lords," said a leech-collector beside a pond.

They slept little, and ate cheese and barley-loaf they bought from cottagers along the way.

"Oh, Nottingham's a day off, my lords," said a matronly woman in a rough-spun apron, shielding her eyes to get a good look at two returning Crusaders. "And God keep you safe," she added, "from the prince's men."

"Are they so very dangerous?" asked Hubert with a carefree-sounding laugh.

"As every soul knows, my lords," said the matron. "Aye, and they're not far behind you even now, judging by the way the birds fall silent through the woodland."

Three days passed.

The two knights parted company, Hubert heading off

toward Bakewell, just a short journey away. Edmund was bound for his old home, and it seemed to him that the hoof-beats sounded out the name of the city, *Nottingham, Nottingham*, just as the jingling bridle chimed *Elviva, Elviva*.

At last Edmund stood in the hall of a great house.

The knight was not tired—an unpleasant shock had just now struck all the weariness from his body.

"I had to ask the guards at the city gates," Edmund found the power to say, "where you were dwelling."

"I am glad," Elviva responded, her voice little more than a whisper, "that they were courteous enough to show you the way."

Servants in tunics of blue indigo passed by the doorway beyond, making a show of rearranging the linen on the table, applying a cloth to a brass candlestick, contriving all the while, Edmund sensed, to eavesdrop excitedly.

"They pulled me along, lane by lane, a whole gathering of welcoming faces," Edmund said, with what he hoped was appropriate courtesy. It was a miracle, he knew, that he could make a sound, as stunned as he was at what he had found in this splendid limestone-and-mortar house.

After identifying himself to the initially skeptical gate-keepers, Edmund had found increasing jubilation in the people he met. Guards called out the tidings to household-er and tavern keeper alike, and happy voices were raised.

"It's Edmund, back from Crusade!" cried more than one person the knight remembered well from his childhood.

It had touched him to hear the familiar accents of folk who had known his parents, and despite his mud-spattered weariness he had felt new strength in his step. No Crusader had yet returned to this part of England, and every question was a version of: Had King Richard captured Jerusalem?

The guards had, it was true, used a degree of circumspection in describing Elviva's new abode, and now Edmund understood why.

The young woman certainly looked much like the Elviva of old, but in many subtle ways she had altered. She was arrayed in brilliantly embroidered clothing, a grander gown than she ever would have worn before. It was blue, with a cunning pattern of wood roses stitched all the way down the flowing *skyrtes*, the trailing part of her garment. She had the familiar green eyes, but her features had undergone some subtle and thorough alteration, her face growing more round and her skin more pale.

This house was new, a dwelling with high stone archways and a rare stone-paved floor, gracefully strewn with sweet-scented rushes. In a city of timber buildings, this was unmistakably the home of a wealthy man—a man with treasure to defend. There would be a cellar, Edmund guessed, with a strongbox of silver. Most dwellings in Edmund's experience did not have separate chambers, but were composed of one large hall around a fireplace. This building had a staircase, step by step leading up into evening shadow. The place was so new that a few of the limestone blocks were still marked with mason's chalk.

Walter fitz Walter himself stood beside a brazier, an

iron tub of glowing coals, and offered a smile more hopeful than happy, looking sideways at Edmund. He was a tall thin man in a mantle of fine white lamb's wool, and he stood very still.

"My father did convince me, Edmund, during his last illness," Elviva was saying. Her voice was familiar but at the same time not as he remembered it. "Just before he died prayerfully last All Saints' Day. Father told me that most regrettably you would likely perish on Crusade, like so many other brave men."

"I am grieved to hear of the death of Peter de Holm," said Edmund, thankful that courteous formula provided conversational stepping-stones. It was considered unlucky to speak of the dead with anything but Christian good manners. "I always admired your father," Edmund added, truthfully enough.

Walter made a prayerful gesture, his hands pressed together, and parted his lips, about to speak.

Elviva gave Walter a long, silencing glance.

More than a year had passed since the days when Edmund had first traveled with Sir Nigel and Sir Rannulf toward London and the Crusades. He had sent no word home to Elviva, and had heard no hint of life in Nottingham—but only castle seneschals and Exchequer's men sent routine messages from one place to another. Edmund knew the truth of what Elviva was saying—many men had died on the Crusade.

"My father," Elviva continued after a pause, "had never assented to my possible marriage to you, Edmund."

The young knight felt a surge of emotion thicken his tongue, and was aware of the curious eyes and ears of servants in the room beyond.

"Walter made a generous wedding payment," Elviva continued, with a visible effort to keep her voice steady. "And my mother was grateful."

"And yet you are happy to see me alive?" asked Edmund, feeling more bitter and helpless with every heartbeat.

"Beyond happy," said Elviva breathlessly. "I am grateful to Heaven for bringing you home again."

Was that, Edmund wondered, a tear in her eye—and a glint of alarm in the eye of her husband? The young knight was certain that the soft-handed husband had never whetted a sword or fastened on a helmet in his life.

Edmund had seen enough of the world to realize that he could seize Elviva and carry her away. It would be a crime, and the sheriff would make Edmund answer for it, but many a townsman would agree that a returning Crusader could be forgiven a bit of passion.

Grab her and carry her like a trussed ewe, urged a secret, war-hardened part of his soul.

Pick her up, and march her right on out through that big oak door.

After all, it's plain that's what she wants.

12

EDMUND CLENCHED HIS FISTS AND STOOD right where he was.

"We are all," Walter fitz Walter was saying, "grateful to Our Lady for bringing you safely home."

Edmund had to admit, privately, that the merchant had a pleasant voice.

"I myself always spoke well of you," Walter added.

He was a respected wine dealer, and had been for years. In a trade marked with shipments of doctored wine—colored with flower petals and flavored with alum and ox blood—a wine merchant who sold an honest beverage was highly valued. Such a man could afford fine clothing and a spit-roasted capon at every midday meal.

"Why should any man speak of me at all?" asked Edmund, just a trace of challenge in his voice.

"I think some might have suspected," returned Walter, "that you were not entirely innocent of your master's crimes."

Elviva spun and gave her husband such a look that the rich man turned away and found some reason to stir the coals in the brazier until sparks spun upward.

But Walter had intended to insult Edmund, and he had succeeded.

I could cut him into chops, thought Edmund, and no man of heart could blame me.

"It was never my pleasure to know you well, good Walter," Edmund found it in himself to say. "But I understand that you provide a fine red wine to the gentlefolk of this town—" Edmund steadied himself, nearly choking on this artful speech. "And I trust that you will provide for the happiness of Elviva."

Walter turned back again, but avoided meeting his wife's eyes. "She has won my heart," he said, a phrase gentlefolk used instead of saying "I love her."

Edmund said nothing further for a moment, wishing Hubert were here to utter something smart but polite.

"You thrived on your Crusade, it would seem," added the wine merchant.

"I was not killed," assented Edmund, "by Heaven's grace."

Edmund was aware that, although he had shaken out his surcoat, and hurriedly washed his face and hands at the well near Goose Gate, he traveled without a squire to polish his leather and wash out his garments. He could not cut much of a figure in the house of such a rich man and, not for the first time in his life, Edmund felt large and coarse— the son of a barrel maker.

The sword at Edmund's side, however, had caught Walter's eye.

"It is plain to see," continued Walter, "that you have received some honor for your efforts."

Edmund's customary modesty made him lower his gaze. "It is true," he agreed. Such things were, in the event, hard to put into words.

"Some soldier's recognition, perhaps?" prompted Elviva in a rapt tone.

Edmund gave a nod.

"Some duke or foreign nobleman paid you a prize?" offered Walter.

"As it pleased Heaven," allowed Edmund, "I was made a knight."

"Edmund!" gasped Elviva.

"By our own Prince John," added Edmund, feeling a stew of pride and embarrassment.

Modesty prompted Edmund to add, "Sir Hubert of Bakewell—my good friend—is a better swordsman than I will ever be. Now *he's* a worthy knight indeed!"

"Sir Edmund, you will dine with us tonight," said Walter fitz Walter fervently.

Having a knight at his table, Edmund knew, would do his household honor.

13

EDMUND EXCUSED HIMSELF FROM THE wine merchant's house without tasting food or drink—although he was hungry, and thirsty, too.

Maud, the widow of Otto the moneyer—Edmund's former master—had remarried. She now lived as the wife of Aymer le Goff, and her husband prospered as chief mason of Nottingham, with an appointment to maintain the city walls. Edmund was heartened at this news—a new husband was often the only means a widow had to provide for her future.

Maud welcomed Edmund with joyful tears, and Aymer called out into the street to come and "see the returning warrior, defender of Jesus!"

Edmund had dreamed of homecoming, but of a different kind, every beloved face in its familiar place. The young knight was increasingly in need of quiet so that he could sort through his tangled feelings.

Aymer insisted on showing Edmund around the fine, stout-timbered dwelling Maud now called her own. It was a prosperous house, with a solar-room for spending pleasant hours with family and guests, and separate bedchambers for the many daughters from Aymer's previous marriage.

"You'll live here with us, dear Edmund, won't you?" pleaded Maud. "And eat stewed mutton and figs every noon—that used to be your favorite."

"And we'll find some dimpled pink-cheeked lass to wed and bed you, Sir Edmund," Aymer joined in heartily.

Aymer's daughters peered through the doorway, too awed to make a sound.

"They've never seen a Crusading knight," Aymer explained. "Not one who has spilled pagan guts."

All five little girls shrank at these words.

Edmund begged leave for himself, saying that he wished to offer his prayers in the parish sanctuary.

Edmund wandered the familiar lanes under a starry sky, bumping his head more than once on an overhanging eave. He had grown taller, or perhaps the town had grown small.

The crooked byways of Nottingham looked as he had remembered them, but they smelled, more strongly than he had recalled, of both human and animal ordure. Had the thatched roofs always appeared so mildewed, even by moonlight? Had these thin, furtive cats always lurked behind dung heaps, and had the pigs feeding on refuse outside dwellings always bickered so loudly?

He had offers of a soft bed in many a noble house, including the sheriff's castle where, the page boy assured him, "every manner of sweet nourishment was being readied." Men and women called out cheerfully to him as he passed.

Edmund smiled and returned greetings, and he accepted more than a few swallows of offered ale, the brown, thick drink he had dreamed of, better than the brew of any other town. Tavern owners pressed food upon him, fish pies and smoked eel, grilled suckers—young rabbits—and fat golden cheese.

Edmund felt, however, that the city indeed had diminished and that the peaked roofs, the chimneys, and even the parish churches were all smaller than he had remembered. Long after the last welcoming matron ceased to call after him, the town subsiding into sleep, Edmund walked the many passages between shops and dwellings, and the night watch let him wander with a chuckling, "Welcome home, Edmund."

Now when the young knight stood still, he was certain he heard the rhythmic chime of chain mail. A booted foot splashed a puddle.

Someone was following.

When Edmund paused to rub the head of a street dog— had these creatures always been so scrawny?—the brindled mutt peered down at the distant hulking shapes of horses in the stable beyond and stiffened, sniffing the air.

"Who's coming after me, like a velvet-footed weasel?" inquired Edmund of the cur, almost believing the creature could speak. What nature of enemy, Edmund wondered, could insinuate his way through the city gates, and past the night watch?

Some enemy.

Some furtive enemy, subtle as the Devil.

Edmund crouched and waited.

A mouse scampered over Edmund's foot, and a night-creature—a bat or an owl—half flew and half fell across the stars. The knight had learned around Crusader camp-fires that no swordsman loves a city fight, where crowded walls secrete enemies and prevent a free swing of the blade.

He crept onward along the street. It was with a feeling of relief that Edmund found the stables, and located Surefoot.

If there was going to be any fighting tonight, thought Edmund, it would be on horseback.

The horse was feeding on a trough of summer grass, and he welcomed Edmund with a gentle nicker.

The stored-up grasses of the previous sunny season—mostly brome and meadow catsfoot—gave the stable a sweet scent, and the horse gave off pleasant animal heat against the increasing night chill. The good-hearted crea-ture reminded Edmund of another horse, one Edmund had loved well—brave Winter Star, mortally injured during the same battle that had so badly stricken Sir Nigel.

Edmund stroked Surefoot. He was speaking to the ani-mal in a soft voice, when the horse shot up its head and gave a snort of warning.

14

A LIGHT TREMBLED AT THE FAR END OF THE stables.

A smoky candle was held aloft by the half-seen arm of a figure wearing what appeared to be a sword and riding-armor, a leather chest piece with a chain-mail skirt.

"My lord?" queried a youthful voice.

Edmund was unaccustomed to the respect routinely offered a knight. For a moment he was convinced that this approaching man-at-arms must have mistaken him for someone else. "If you are looking for Edmund, the former moneyer's apprentice," he responded at last, "you have found him."

Then he had to laugh silently at the sound of his own voice. He used to overhear gruff, sword-wearing men on market day in years gone by and marvel at their rough manner. Now Edmund himself had turned into one of them, and he did not entirely relish the transformation.

"My lord, if it please you," said a youth with wax-yellow hair, little more than a boy. "I have a word for your ears."

"If you have come to put me in chains," said Edmund,

speaking with a calm, defiant frankness, "you will need companions."

"My lord, I have a duty to you," said the young man, "and a bitter message." He sank to his knees in a show of obeisance. His hand was trembling, the light sending quaking shadows throughout the stable. "One I have been reluctant to deliver, if you'll forgive me."

"What knight do you serve, good squire?" said Edmund.

"My lord, I serve you," said the boy. "If you would allow it."

Edmund considered this. "Who sends you to me?"

"My lady Elviva," was the reply. "She said I'd make a better squire than house servant, and I will prove her right."

Edmund directed the lad to stand up.

"My lord," continued the boy, "the gate guards are loyal to King Richard, and will not let the prince's men set foot in town. But the report from messengers is that the usurper's men have captured Sir Rannulf."

"What messengers carry such tidings?"

"Woodsmen, Sir Edmund—outlaws, if you please, but not the cutthroat variety. Men who have little love for Prince John."

"These rough men must be mistaken."

"And my lord," added the lad reluctantly, "Prince John's men have offended our cause all the further by capturing Sir Nigel."

Edmund struck the stable wall a blow with his fist.

Horses stirred all around, nickering and turning in their shelters.

"And, my lord, forgive me for reporting so," said the boy, all but sinking to his knees again, "these green-clad men say that the prince's followers have taken Sir Hubert captive, too."

Edmund wrapped his hand around the pommel of his sword. *Heaven be my shield.* "Is there any further news you have for me?" asked Edmund, with a great effort at calm.

"My name is Wowen Wight, my lord," said the squire. "My father was scutifer to old Sir Roger of this town, and he was a patient teacher. I think you'll find I can tell a spear from a spoon."

A scutifer was a shield bearer, an additional assistant employed by many knights. Edmund had known the late Sir Roger by sight and reputation, and had seen Wowen's father, Azo, winning bets as a wrestler on many a market day.

"The prince's men have set up camp across Lazar Field," reported Wowen, "grilling a doe from the king's woods. If it pleases you to fight Prince John's hirelings," added Wowen, "I'll be honored to battle at your side."

These words gave Edmund a certain involuntary thrill. "Fighting is not the stuff you've heard in songs," he said. How gruff I sound, Edmund thought—like a grizzled knight. Much, in truth, like Sir Nigel or Sir Rannulf before they had their ale and mutton at day's end.

"My father did not raise a simpleton, my lord," said Wowen. "Or a coward."

"How old are you, squire?" asked Edmund.

"I have seen thirteen winters, my lord," he replied, growing just a bit taller at being called *squire*. "I can use a knife as well as any skinner."

Edmund felt his own lack of experience keeping him where he was, in the security of the warm stable. This large, holy sword was a boon, but just then he needed Nigel's advice, and Hubert's quick eye.

"Sleepy men can barely fight," offered Wowen, with the assurance of a novice.

He added, "Let's surprise them."

15

EDMUND WAITED UNTIL THE PREDAWN hush, watching from a place with the *woge gard*—the wall guard—from a perch high above Goose Gate.

"Look at that—see them pass around another wineskin, Sir Edmund," said one of the guards, pointing with a gnarled finger across the moon-bleached field where cooking fires subsided, and the sounds of talk and song grew quiet.

"They don't look much like fighting men," said Edmund thoughtfully.

"I count five sets of helmets and shields," advised the guard. "And more than a dozen spear carriers, none of them as fit as King Richard's men used to be. It's a sad thing, to see a king's brother putting armor on England's tavern dregs."

"No sign of their prisoners?" asked Edmund.

"No, my lord," was the answer.

"In readying an attack," Nigel had once counseled, "you wait, and then you wait. And after that, you begin to wait."

Edmund waited.

"The roosters will stir before long," advised Wowen.

The city gate whispered open at last.

Edmund urged his mount forward through the starlit field.

Surefoot was happy to race Wowen's mount, a sleek, black mare with a single splash of white on one foreleg. Surefoot was what horsemen called an entire—a stallion. While Surefoot had always been energetic, the presence of the mare made the spotted silver-and-gray male eager to show off his speed.

The drowsy prince's men did not see them coming, until Surefoot snorted and kicked among them.

True enough, only one sentry had been posted, and even from horseback Edmund could smell the wine on his breath. Edmund drew his sword, but hesitated to use the weapon against a clumsy fellow countryman. The heavy-footed spearman offered a halfhearted jab with his spear, and Edmund let his own suppressed bitterness give strength to his counterattack.

The young knight raised his foot from the stirrup and kicked his opponent in the head. The footman fell back, arms wheeling, until he collapsed in a pile of saddle blankets.

Edmund cut a great arc out of the air, the blade making a sharp song. Footmen let their weapons fall as Edmund demanded, "Where are my companions?"

Only one knight climbed into his saddle, a bushy-haired man. He sawed heavily at the reins, trying to wrestle his mount around to face the attack. Surefoot approached the startled horse and, with no prompting from Edmund, took a bite out of the alarmed animal's mane.

Wowen darted close on the other side of the shaggy-haired knight and made a sawing back-and-forth with his knife at the knight's saddle girth, cutting it through. Wowen gave a tug at the knight's arm, and the man tumbled from his horse—followed by his saddle.

Edmund leaned down from his mount and put the point of his sword into the shaken knight's wispy chin, just firmly enough to prick the skin.

"If you have hurt my friends," said Sir Edmund, "by the saints—"

Edmund stopped the onward rush of his words. He had been given to rash vows in the past, and now, with this holy weapon in his grasp, he realized the weight of his threats.

Chop them all up, urged an inner, spiteful voice in Edmund's heart. Scatter them for the flesh-crows.

Edmund drew a long breath. Of all the virtues, Edmund knew, God most prized mercy.

A group of quickly dressed footmen and disheveled knights rode beside Edmund and Wowen through the breaking dawn.

The woolly-haired knight introduced himself as Neville of Eu, and he spoke in tones of businesslike gentility as he dabbed at his chin with a wad of folded linen. Sir Neville remarked, with an air of jovial wariness and a heavy Frankish accent, "If you intend to free your fellow Crusaders, Sir Edmund, you will find yourself greatly outnumbered."

Edmund made no answer.

It was correct for Sir Neville and the spearmen to ride quietly with Edmund. They had given their word that they would be peaceful—and besides, they were close to another, larger band of Prince John's men and had little fear of Edmund and his squire.

The road was a swath of dark, spring-damp mud, pounded and gouged by hoof and cart. When a sentry's warning sang out, "Saint George and Prince John!" the shaggy knight responded, "Prince John and Our Lady!" As the phalanx of riders entered a well-ordered camp, morning wine was being warmed over a merry fire.

All around Edmund, twenty men buckled sword belts and fitted on helmets in the glow of the sunrise. The young knight nearly laughed, given the absurd odds against him, but he recalled all the tales he had heard of solitary knights taking on a score of fighters. Such bold men-at-arms were always cut down, in both history and song, but not before nine or ten of their opponents writhed on strife-torn soil.

Edmund recognized that he and Wowen were trapped. There would be no easy escape.

He realized that Hubert would have been capable of some cunning act, and that Rannulf would have scattered men to the right and to the left.

But Edmund wanted more than anything to see his companions again. He said, simply, "Show me to my friends."

16

AS ONE NIGHT EBBED INTO ANOTHER, ESTER rarely interrupted her vigil at her father's side.

Reginald proved his worth as a physician, looking in on his patient several times during both day and nighttime hours, and often brought something to brighten Ester's long wait—Valencia oranges or Poitevin peaches. Such fruit was rare. The Crusades had taken up most of the freight vessels throughout Christendom, and what shipping remained was increasingly harried by pirates.

"The doctor seeks to snare you in his net," said Ida.

"I barely notice him," said Ester, "except to discuss my father's health."

"The bee spies the hedge rose," said Ida, employing a well-worn conversational motif, "whether the blossom notices or not."

Bernard drifted into a restless sleep, shivering and muttering. At times he parted his eyelids, only to look around as if at some unholy place, startled, unaware of his surroundings.

At the sound of his daughter's voice, however, his anxiety always subsided. "Have some warm hippocras," she urged—spiced wine, yet another gift from Reginald. Bernard drank, and while he did not stir beyond a few moments of wakefulness, neither did he drift again into unfathomed torpor.

"Is there reason for hope?" Ester asked one evening, stopping the doctor at the doorway, one hand on his sleeve.

Reginald took her hand.

During one of Father Catald's visits, Ester reminded the priest of her pilgrim's vow.

"We don't bargain with Heaven, Ester," he reflected with a meditative smile.

He had brought her six pears, a remnant from last autumn's harvest and still unbruised. The little priest remained standing in the center of the room, his hands tucked into his sleeves. "We can strike no agreement with Our Lord," he said, repeating his counsel.

His eyes were full of unspoken meaning—as though he was about to add "And yet."

"In my prayers tonight," said the priest, "I'll remind Heaven of your vow."

One evening Ester was mending her father's slipper by the light of a single candle.

The feel of the thimble gently rasping against the needle was pleasing, a sense of small but definite effort making a torn thing whole again. His favorite leather slippers had been brightly colored. Many times she had offered to repair them, but he had insisted, "Some things are better as they are."

So she was not listening, nor paying full heed, when his bare foot slipped down out of the bedding, followed by the other. Only when he was standing did she realize what was happening, and she stood herself, letting her mending fall to the floor.

Bernard ran a hand over his head, arranged the folds of his gown, and walking—a little shakily, but taking a tall man's strides. He reached the plate on which the six glowing pears were still in their prime.

"They *are* real," he said, with a quiet laugh.

"Father Catald brought them," was all Ester could say.

"I thought they were a vision," said Bernard.

He took a bite, and closed his eyes in pleasure.

17

HUBERT PACED THE WIDE, STONE-PAVED floor.

"Don't worry yourself, good Hubert," said Nigel. "We'll see you all the way to Rome, and into the Lady Galena's arms."

"At what risk to each of you?" asked Hubert. "It would be safer for you to stay here in England."

"And serve the prince?" interjected Edmund.

Hubert sighed and shook his head.

Edmund felt deep compassion for his friend, and he was nursing a secret plan—a scheme that included overpowering the guards, surmounting the Tower walls, and hiding in a merchant ship along the wharf. He admitted to himself, however, that the details of the plan needed further work.

The trip back to London had been one of honorable arrest, as was appropriate when knights took their social equals into custody. Rannulf had nothing to say, and Nigel accepted his capture as a temporary matter to be, as he put it to the prince's men, "resolved through a bribe or an act of God."

The swelling troop of sergeants, barely competent knights, and assorted pikemen, had guarded their wards with care but every courtesy. The three-day journey back to London and the stone fortress and prison of the Tower had been marked by their captors' curiosity and increasing respect as Nigel described the siege of Acre.

"We will travel back to Rome," Nigel was saying now, "because it is our duty under Heaven."

Hubert made a gesture of exasperation. He had been able to see neither home nor family, and now ran his hands through his hair like a young man at the very limits of anguish and disgrace.

"Our Lady will not abandon us, Hubert," Edmund said.

Hubert gave a worried nod.

Their sojourn in a large chamber in the Tower had so far lasted only one night and half a day, and it had been far from unpleasant. While it was true that guards stood outside the door, the knights had dined on smoked river pike and roast piglet, and as much prized white bread as they could eat. They had been allowed to keep their weapons— a gesture of high courtesy—but Sir Robert de Tuit, steward to the king, had asked the knights to swear that they would not use their swords. They were guests, and at the same time they were prisoners.

A few more knights had begun to return from the Crusade in recent days, war-scarred men with no taste for further strife, nor with news of major victories. These homebound warriors were generally loyal to Richard, and

Tower guards had shared the rumor that Nigel, Rannulf, and the two new knights might be liberated by an armed band of former Crusaders.

Now Edmund was quick to reassure Hubert that they would find Galena well and true in her love for Hubert. Nevertheless, Edmund felt the stirring of a private doubt— what was to keep Galena from falling in love, or even marrying, in the many months before any of them could see Rome again?

Edmund was pleased to see that Wowen could burnish a sword, showing a deft hand with a whetstone. The squire took a boyish wonder in daggers and cutting weapons generally. Edmund showed him how to repair a spur that Rannulf had nearly lost in the forest, mending the leather and putting a new point on the single goad.

A few times on the journey back to London, and here in their comfortable prison, Edmund had found his voice lifted in song. It was not unusual for a fighting man to sing, or to lift a pious prayer, or to burst into tears at the sight of a crucifix or the image of Our Lady. But Edmund had never before been given to such prayerful songs as "O Sweet and Holy Wound" or "Our Lady, Heal My Longing."

Even now, Edmund was singing softly, only half aware of the sound as he polished the leather of his own spur.

"I do believe," said Nigel with an affectionate smile, "that our friend Sir Edmund suffers greater heartache than he will admit."

The iron-studded oak door gave a rattle.

A key was worked into the lock, and when the door swung inward a page boy strode into the room. He was pale, and the flush in his cheeks betrayed high feeling.

"Worthy lords," he began, his glance darting from man to man.

"Speak your piece, lad," prompted Nigel with good cheer.

"My lord Prince John sends word that he will see you now."

The page appeared about to say something more.

"What more," asked Nigel, "do you have to tell us?"

"My lords, the prince allows me to tell you that he continues displeased." *Dysplesed*.

"He has kept us mewed up for a full day, and another until nearly evening," said Nigel mildly. "Like his pet hawks, punished for their mischief."

The page appeared torn between a sworn duty and some other feeling. The boy perhaps took heart at the sight of Wowen, a lad nearly his own age. "My lords, you may not take your swords."

The four knights left Wowen behind and walked with a dozen black-leather-clad guards across a grassy courtyard.

These men did not respond to Nigel's question, "Is that a magpie among the ravens?" nor did they make any other utterance, marching the four captive knights to a broad door.

They waited a long time before the iron-studded barrier, blackbirds making their crazed, musical laughter overhead, while Edmund's optimism began to fade. As unarmed knights they felt essentially naked, and Edmund realized how foolish he had been to dream of escape.

"What is there to keep the prince," asked Edmund in a low voice, "from separating our heads from our bodies?"

"Why would he do that?" asked Nigel.

"Ill humor," suggested Edmund.

"Edmund, if our noble prince suffers a homicidal whim," Nigel responded with a dry chuckle, "not one of us is safe."

The surrounding walls were high. The wall guard was well armored, nine men gazing down at the four Crusaders with an air of curiosity. More than one carried a large, double-headed ax.

18

THE PRINCE SAT SILENT AS THE CRUSADERS knelt.

Prince John gave no sign of knowing they were there, and this troubled Edmund very much. The longer the prince's silence endured, the more clearly the knight could sense the proud man's displeasure.

The meeting room was bare, except for a large oaken chair, occupied by Prince John. The prince wore a bright orpiment-gold mantle, a color so expensive some called it "king's yellow." In addition to his brilliant topaz ring, the king wore a kidney-red jasper amulet, cunningly engraved with the lance and dragon of Saint George. The king's brother studied a scroll, a list of numbers and words.

It was unusual to see a man reading silently. Most readers murmured as they read, or read the words out in a clear voice. The prince made an absentminded gesture, ordering them to stand, but he did not take his eyes off the black letters before him. Edmund was all too aware of his own stature, the tallest figure in the room. If only I could shrink.

At last, with a show of indifference, Prince John left his seat, handed the document to a servant, and wandered across the room to a shuttered window. As he did so, he deliberately turned his back on the four knights. It was considered an insult for a prince to turn his back on men of quality during a formal interview, and Nigel lifted his gaze briefly toward Heaven.

John opened the shutter a finger-width and peered at the world outside.

Late afternoon sunlight lanced into the chamber, and for a long time the prince seemed lost in the musical, throaty call of a distant woodcock. A drift of sweet wind slipped into the room.

"My lord prince," said Nigel, in a tone weighted with respect, "if it is possible for a knight to dare to inquire—why have you asked to see us?"

Nigel's question was abrupt, and although delivered artfully, was close to being impertinent—or dangerous. Even an accomplished knight like Nigel did not ask a direct question to a prince. John ignored the silver-haired men-at-arms, closed the shutter gently, and made his way back to his high-backed chair. He took a long moment to select a pear from a brightly polished silver bowl.

"I myself," said the prince at last, "did not want to set eyes on you." His gaze cut to one side, and Edmund felt the princely gaze take him in, weigh him, dismiss him. And look back again.

The prince added, "Someone else desired to see you. Someone whose interests I am bound to respect."

A distant rustling sound, and quiet womanly voices, began to approach from outside.

The prince instantly stiffened in his chair, and brushed the front of his mantle with his hand. The castle guards along the wall stiffened, too, their eyes locked straight ahead.

Edmund's pulse began to race at the approaching whispers.

The unmistakable process of a very important personage was heralded outside by a flurry of activity in the garden.

A servant plied a broom across a footpath in what sounded like a hurried—indeed, frantic—manner, and pikemen strode unseen somewhere outside, their leather creaking and their boots, in careful rhythm, growing ever closer. Some noble soul was approaching, with a rustle of clothing and the soft whisper of expensive footwear.

As the door opened, Nigel and Rannulf threw themselves onto the floor in obeisance, and Hubert and Edmund joined them.

Edmund turned his head just enough to observe the sweeping skirts of a grand lady enter the room.

19

"ARISE, CRUSADER KNIGHTS, SO I CAN SEE you," said a woman's voice—a well-spoken Frankish command.

She entered with several young women, all garbed in flowing sleeves and rustling silk gowns. No household but a queen's had so many female attendants. Edmund stood as he was directed, but he could not look in the royal person's direction, and he hoped he would not have to speak a word. Edmund was aware, too, of the travel-worn figure they all cut, garbed in faded Crusader surcoats.

The prince vacated his chair, and as his mother sat, her son strolled over to the window, examining the untasted pear in his hand.

The queen took a moment to survey the men before her.

"So you are Sir Rannulf of Josselin," said Queen Eleanor at last, looking at the veteran knight appraisingly.

Sir Rannulf was unable to respond, except to kneel before her. "My lady queen," rasped Rannulf.

"Arise, arise," she responded, with a motion of her hand and a nearly manly chuckle.

Rannulf did as he was told, and the queen leaned forward and said, "They tell me that no enemy is safe from you, worthy knight."

"My lady queen, they speak too well of me," said Rannulf when he could make a sound. Through his scarred lips he spoke in a rapt tone Edmund had never heard from the knight before.

She sat back and studied the four of them once more. "All of you fought under my son in the Holy Land," she said. It was a declaration, not a question, but only Nigel understood what the royal lady wanted to hear.

"My lady queen," he said, "our lord king was well in body and spirit, and blessed by Heaven with victories."

"But he had not captured Jerusalem," said the queen.

This remark needed no response. At last tidings, the Holy City remained in pagan hands.

"And the lice and the heat rash got the better of all of you," she said, not unkindly. "And the flux, cramps, and fever striking half the army, black water squirting from the guts of half the footmen. I know what war is like. But by God, I wish I had been there to see the army of Jesus! What was it like, young knight?"

She was looking right at Edmund, with eyes that were dark brown and golden at once.

She was beautiful as well-loved silver is beautiful, with gray hair and pale skin. Edmund could not speak. He shaped an inner prayer to Saint Michael, provider of strength, and then he heard his voice like an utterance from another room, "My lady queen, we fought—"

Words fled.

Edmund was losing all power of communication. He gathered his will, but still could make no further sound.

Hubert whispered at his side, prompting him.

Edmund added, repeating Hubert's words, "We fought as Heaven gave us the power."

The queen smiled.

When he could breathe again, Edmund felt that he had passed through an ordeal as challenging as battle, and lifted a silent prayer of thanks.

He allowed his gaze to wander briefly.

To his surprise he recognized one of the members of the royal company—the young woman whose father had been hurt in the melee. And she recognized Edmund—there could be no mistaking that flicker in her emerald eyes.

Without being fully aware of it, Edmund had determined to never look at another woman as long as he lived. He would not be as absolute as Rannulf, who mistrusted and even disliked the sex. But in the wake of his meeting with Elviva, Edmund had a vague impression that he himself would be more like a Templar knight, a man with kindly feelings toward women, but sworn to avoid them.

Despite this sincere inclination, he could not keep an expression of welcome—and even friendliness—from his gaze for a moment. The young woman responded with something like a smile, until a sense of duty recaptured her attention.

"I have a charge for you to undertake," said the queen.

Not one of the four knights could make a sound, although Hubert made the sign of the cross and Nigel gave a bow.

"My son John, at my request, will send you to Rome," the queen added, with no further preamble.

"My lady queen!" said Nigel, a gasp of both astonishment and joy.

"You will," said the queen, "leave at once."

Edmund sensed Hubert trembling joyfully beside him.

"The prince," added the queen, "will give you license to take the horses you require."

The royal lady cocked her head to address the prince. "You will keep these men from journeying like naked kerns to the town of the lord pope, will you not, John?" Kerns were Irish and Scottish foot soldiers of no great reputation and legendary shabbiness.

"As the queen wishes," replied the prince—with every sign of gentle agreement.

"You will take with you, Christian knights," the queen continued, "an esteemed young lady and member of my household. She is going on a pilgrimage, to pray in the holy sites of Rome."

She added, in a voice both sweet to the ear and commanding, "You will defend her with your honor—and your lives."

II
Soldier Pilgrims

20

PRINCE JOHN SAT IN THE HIGH-ARMED OAK
chair.

He was oblivious to the guards nearby, alive only to his
own thoughts.

He held the pear still untasted in his hand. His mother,
the four crusaders, and the flock of ladies had all just then
departed, leaving the faint but definite scent of attar of
roses in the room. His mother bathed in the stuff, which she
could not actually afford.

The prince gave a quiet, dry laugh. He put a knuckle to
his teeth, and bit. He bit hard, but not hard enough to draw
blood, he saw when he examined the indentations in his skin.

He would do as his mother wished and let the four
knights depart the kingdom. It was as well to please his
mother, who was some seventy years old and no doubt
would not live much longer. And he had his own reasons
for wanting the four wayward knights out of the realm.

He resented them, and now wished them dead—two
youthful knights who felt no gratitude, and two weathered
knights who dared to challenge John's will. Such men were
dangerous, and encouraged others. If a rooster woke a

prince, its neck was broken. If a fighting man offended, you set him a dangerous foe.

John was a proud man, and jealous. England did not know it, Prince John brooded, but she needed a ruler of his foresight and ability. Why were Richard's fighting men so devoted to their wayward king?

"Send for Sir Jean de Chartres," said the prince, bitterness forcing his voice to a whisper.

The page bowed, as these Londoners were taught to bow. It was an awkward sight, like watching a piglet prop its body up on its crooked little hindquarters and try to dance.

The sight very nearly moved one to pity.

Jean de Chartres knelt before the prince.

The prince said, "Would you like to taste one of these fine pears?"

A member of the royal family rarely offered a knight any such morsel, and the Chartrian's eyes were bright with both gratitude and caution.

The big knight's hand closed around the yellow fruit in John's palm, the pear warm from the prince's touch.

The prince made a gesture, and the footmen filed out of the room, leaving the prince and the knight alone.

"It was a shame the way that upstart Hubert killed Sir Nicholas," said the prince. "He learned foul fighting from that murderer Rannulf."

"My lord prince," said the Chartrian, both compliant and mystified, setting aside the pear as a prize. "It was all done as Heaven desired."

"No, I believe that those four knights are dangerous," the prince allowed himself to say. "They fight like felons— and laugh in their prayers. I was mistaken to elevate the two squires to knighthood, and now I would obliterate my error."

"I have no reason to show them mercy," said the Chartrian. "But I am reconciled to God's will."

That was well said enough, thought Prince John with little pleasure. "I would be happy, and generous in my joy," the prince continued with a trace of impatience, "if the four knights did not reach Rome."

"My lord prince, I would please you," said the big knight. "But I would obey more easily if I fully knew your desire."

The prince saw that the knight was cunning enough to need explicit orders. John leaned close, putting his lips by the big man's ear. "Travel with as many men as you need."

Sir Jean nodded, too excited to speak.

"Employ a well-mounted army," continued the prince, sitting back but continuing to speak in a low voice. "That is what you'll require, to kill these men."

"My lord prince," began the knight, as eager to bargain as any housewife, "I look forward to my reward for this service to you."

Only a Chartrian would put the matter so coarsely, thought the prince. Money was as important to a knight as to any man, but what a knight of real ambition sought was to be promoted to the ranks of the *milites de familia regis*— knights of the royal household.

"I am sending the four knights and their lady charge by

way of the Alps," the prince said. "Seagoing ships are few, and the mountain route can be quicker for capable travelers. See that they lose their lives in some wasteland, where no one will associate our person with the bloodshed—and not on English soil."

Besides, thought the prince, if Sir Jean failed, some alpine brigand might well finish the job. Or perhaps a tumble of mountain boulders, or a killing frost. The route through the alpine pass was tended by a brave band of monks founded by Bernard of Aosta. Many travelers died despite their help.

"My father was Sir Beaumont le Brun, my lord prince," the Chartrian replied in response, "and his father kept a sword that had belonged to King Pepin le Breve."

"You have a family of treasured name," said the prince, regretting that such bargaining could not be left to some steward's clerk. "Bring me back the severed sword hands of the four offending knights, and you'll hold a high station in my court."

If my brother Richard does not return from his Crusade.

Sir Jean of Chartres drew his sword. He knelt before the prince, kissing the hilt of the weapon as a man would kiss the holy cross.

Prince John lifted a finger. "But see," added the prince, "that the young lady Ester completes her pilgrimage to Rome."

It would not be wise to offend Heaven.

21

THE CHANNEL WATERS WERE A STRANGE, liverish color, dark and troubled. Ester told herself she did not mind.

"Why did our Lord God," asked Nigel, "bother making so much water? The oceans are too full of it."

There was a good deal of sea, it was true, and yet Ester began the journey convinced that their pilgrimage was protected by divine will, and that no harm could touch them.

Their travel would take them across the Channel, and then down a landlocked route, through the grape-growing estates of minor barons, toward the life-threatening barrier of the Alps. But Ester was not afraid, she reminded herself. With Ida at her side, in the company of her companion knights, the young lady-in-waiting thrilled at the rocking of the salt-cured cog.

The *Saint Veronica* was a stout-timbered ship, fit for ferrying horses and pilgrim folk across the wind-battered body of salt water between France and England. Ester had voyaged many times before, as a part of the queen's company, and with her father on his way to consult the learned men of Aachen and Paris.

And she had endured hardship in her life before now, too. Despite the artful conversation and well-sung ballads of court life, there had been many days of leathery salt-whiting and watered wine in the castle of the queen. Old King Henry had tended to bicker with his wife, and send her to virtual durance—imprisonment—in pleasant but remote castles. Ester had been a member of the queen's court since her girlhood, and had known days when the noontime meal was nothing but a pigeon's egg and day-old bread.

Now Ester carried an amulet in a soft kidskin pouch, hidden in her clothing. It was the special token that the pope had, years before, given Eleanor—the relic of Saint George. Ester had been cautioned by the queen to keep this holy object secret—it was too valuable and sacred to be exposed rashly.

As the stout ship rose up over the Channel swells, and sank down into the sea trough, Ester blinked back tears of gratitude at the queen's kindness.

They set foot on the sandy shore of France after a voyage of less than two days, and at once set forth along the rutted market paths of Normandy.

It was true that aside from Wowen Wight there were no other squires, but the queen had provided the pilgrims with an experienced retainer from her own household: a burly Kentishman named Clydog, along with two young assistants, Hervey and Eadwin.

Clydog had been a steward to the queen for many years, chastising serving lads with his glance. Ester had seen him straighten the long handle of a waffle iron with his bare hands, and as chief servant on their pilgrimage he could build a fire from a spark and a pinch of damp wood mold, and prepare kettle-poached fish in a pouring rain. If there was one flaw in the man's character, it was that he tended to have a low opinion of any man or woman less capable than he, whether lowborn or high.

Even now, the stalwart retainer was hurrying the travelers up the sandy slope. "Come along now, worthy knights," he said, motioning them onward with an ill-disguised impatience. "Ride steady on your mounts, my ladies," he added, as though without his urging, she and Ida would surely fall off.

Ester and Ida both rode the best palfreys, with soft saddles and leather-bound bridles. The geldings had been bred for travel and they were quick to answer both the rein and the soft word of encouragement. Ester rode astride, as was proper for a traveling lady—only in the most elaborate pageants did a lady ride sidesaddle.

In the passing days, Ester modified her skeptical attitude toward knights.

Sir Rannulf, a darkly bearded man, was a silent figure as weathered as a tanner's boot. He rarely spoke. But he stood sentry at night without complaint, and once Ester woke to see the warrior's scarred visage bending near, as he threw another blanket over her against a sudden night mist.

As they had passed through the fabled town of Gisors, Sir Rannulf traded his moody mount for a fleet horse with a long, graceful neck. On this animal the bearded knight ranged back along the highway they had already traveled, hunting for possible trouble. His sable-brown charger was called Strikefire, and no other horse could run as fast or travel as far.

Sir Nigel of Nottingham she found a knight of pleasing spirits, a man her father would have enjoyed calling a fellow pilgrim. He was quick to laugh, full of pleasure at the sight of children playing football with an ox's bladder, or a flock of swans rising overhead. He did drink more deeply than anyone else from the wineskin, but he was civil to beggars and itinerant songsters, and more than once let a farthing spin into a cripple's cup.

Hubert of Bakewell she liked well, too, a good-natured knight overflowing with talk of his lady-love, who awaited him in Rome. He was quick to goad his friend Edmund into laughter with wry comments and imitations of millers and cowherds they passed. Feelings gave quick color to his cheeks. Such a young man, Ester believed, could never strike a deliberate killing blow. Hubert's victory during the joust must indeed have been an act of Heaven's will and due to no particular fighting skill on his part.

Edmund stirred stronger feelings in her.

He was the one she sought first with her eyes each morning, and last at night, in the flicker of the dying fire. He was bigger than the rest, and often given to quiet song and prayer. Whether he was a sworn man of violence, or a prayerful and gentle soul, she could not decide.

One noon as they rested their mounts, she knelt beside a fast-running stream and drank out of her cupped hand.

"You are wise to do that, my lady," said Edmund, his shadow falling over her.

"To drink water?" Ester asked, half playful, half in doubt regarding his intentions.

It was widely known that to drink still water, from a slow-flowing river or—even worse—a pond, was to court death from cramps and fever. This water was fiercely cold and fast, as though plunging down a long way, from some yet-unseen mountainside.

"To not lower your mouth into the running stream," the tall knight was saying.

"Like a doe, you mean—or a cow," she said, hoping that the play of conversation could win the young knight's regard.

"It's best to be watchful," he said. He spoke English with the accent of the northern shires, musical to her ear if perhaps a little hard to understand at times.

Ester was forced by his remark to glance around at the pleasant scene of grapes heavy on the rows of vines. Peasants walked the vineyards, plying hoes and testing the readiness of the harvest. Yet another pretty little castle, the stronghold of some local family, perched on a modest hill, little more than a tower and a draw-gate. Ester's party had traveled for several weeks through a land where one sort of Frankish or another had been spoken, and they had dined on the most expensive white bread and fat cheese, purchased from the local farmers.

If this was a typical pilgrimage, Ester had begun to think, she did not know why folk considered travel such a hardship.

"Is there a great need of such watchfulness?" she queried.

Edmund gave the question more thought than she had expected. "Rannulf thinks we are being followed," said the knight at last.

Ester admitted to herself that she was ignorant of the world of knighthood, but she was not an innocent. She knew that women of name, and men, too, were sometimes captured and held for ransom.

"You need not guard me like a newborn lamb, Sir Edmund," she replied. "You must think me an unweaned fool."

To her surprise, the comment made the suntanned knight falter, and even blush. "My lady Ester," he said at last, "I would not permit any churl or knight to utter such a slur."

Later that afternoon Rannulf rode hard, catching up with the mounts of his companions.

"There's no mistaking him," said Rannulf. "Sir Jean is riding with five knights, each with a squire and a shield bearer, all hoof-hard. And with enough steel to butcher an army."

22

ESTER MADE AN EFFORT TO HIDE HER ALARM.

Her own party of travelers, while richly dressed and well nourished, was outfitted for a seemly pilgrimage, but not for battle.

Each of them wore a neatly sewn cross near the right shoulder, the traditional insignia of folk on a pilgrimage. Packhorses carried the knights' helmets and shields, but only Rannulf and Hubert were supplied with fighting lances. A pilgrimage to Rome was not a Crusade.

The travelers posted double sentries that night, and when Ester chided them for not thinking that a young woman had eyes and ears, Nigel laughed. He appointed her to help stand the third watch, just before dawn.

She had hoped to stand guard with Edmund, but instead stood guard with Rannulf, a man who often did double watch as a sentry after a long day of travel, as though he did not need sleep.

"No force would attack at night, or am I mistaken?" she asked the darkly bearded knight.

Rannulf stirred, his travel armor making a musical whisper. He considered a long time without speaking.

Ester grew a little weary of waiting.

"I have heard poems of fighting all my life," added Ester, feeling regret now that she had troubled to inquire. "Most war ballads speak of the sunlight off shields and the scarlet scales of the dragon. I never hear of pilgrims being slaughtered."

Rannulf was disturbed at the prospect of speaking to this young lady of quality. He looked on neither man nor woman with desire, but believed that no good came from trading words with a female of any sort.

Nevertheless, Rannulf was loyal to his cohorts, be they squire or lady. More than once he had been careful to see that fire sparks did not breathe harm upon Ester and her lady friend. And he was still touched by the notice Queen Eleanor had given him all those weeks ago. To have a royal lady of such fame and personal dignity speak to him of his own faded triumphs altered Rannulf's view of womankind in subtle ways. He had felt gratitude.

Perhaps this young woman had more than a little of the queen's virtue and grace, he privately admitted. Surely Ester was well spoken, and Rannulf could see no spite or mischief in her—without extending the same confidence to Ida.

And yet, what could he say, with his scarred lips, that would be wise, or strike such a lady—accustomed to conversation with a queen—as remotely polite?

Well, he told himself, he had to say something. Rannulf

gathered his will. Heaven had yet to present him with a challenge he could not equal.

"Harm, my lady," he said at last, "can come at any hour."

A long while passed, and Rannulf gave an inward, stoical sigh. Perhaps conversation was, for him, a too-long neglected art.

Just then a fox across the fields spoke up, a query answered far away by a vixen. It was an alarm, one hunter to another. There was trouble out there under the stars.

23

ALL THE NEXT DAY THEY KEPT THEIR
moderate pace—Nigel had emphasized that sapping the
strength of a horse was cruel to both steed and traveler.

Outwardly, they were the same band of earnest pilgrims, but Ester was aware of little ways in which the
knights betrayed their readiness.

Edmund fell back from time to time, eyeing the road
behind for the approach once again of Rannulf, and Hubert
drew his blade often as he rode, making practice sweeps at
the air.

At last Rannulf rode up, shaking his head.

"I see," said Nigel, "that we have run out of peaceful
hours."

"They are upon us," said his companion-in-arms.

"How much time do we have?" asked Nigel.

"Use your ears," was all Rannulf would say as he let
Strikefire drink from a fast-moving stream.

A flurry of dust far across the vineyards marked the progress of Sir Jean's force. The dust was rising fast, and growing closer with every heartbeat.

Peasants working in the vineyards stood straight and shaded their eyes at the far-off rhythm of hoofbeats. Even the sole pikeman on the nearby fortress tower leaned over the wall to see what was approaching.

Ester had sat at Queen Eleanor's knee, embroidering flower patterns in linen, and heard the queen tell of old King Henry's brave knights, and the bloodthirsty robbers near Constantinople. If there was going to be a fight, Ester would not embarrass herself. Ida put a kerchief to her lips and prayed, gripping her reins so tightly her palfrey took a few steps back.

"They mean to see us hurt, or worse," said Edmund to Ester in a matter-of-fact tone. Edmund gave a gesture to his squire, but the boy had already retrieved some of the armor from a packhorse, and placed a helmet in Edmund's hands.

"But you don't know this for certain," Ester managed to say.

Ida was tugging at her sleeve. "These knights are too few to guard us," she said in a quick monotone.

"These are our brave friends," responded Ester.

Nigel inclined his head toward Edmund for a moment, muttering some advice, and Edmund turned to Ester and her friend with an urgent "Lady Ester, ride with me to that nearby castle."

"Sir Edmund," she said, "I will not fly like the sparrow from the owl."

"My lady, both of you be quick," called Edmund, spurring his mount.

24

THE CASTLE WITH THE SINGLE PIKE CARRIER
was not much more than a tower and a stout oak draw-
gate, the entire structure little larger than a simple country
house.

It was equipped with arrow slits, the tower well
designed, with stone-and-mortar battlements to allow the
sentry shelter from attack. Just now the guard peered out at
them, lifting a hand in a gesture of helplessness.

"Merciful pilgrims," the castle keeper was saying, "God
keep you in gracious peace."

Ester repeated their request for shelter. She understood
now why Edmund had asked the two young women to
appear before the castle. What castle would allow a band of
pilgrim females to suffer injury right outside its door?

"The lord of this keep is still far away, on Crusade,"
replied the guard, a poorly shaven man of meager appearance, missing many of his teeth. "I dare not allow any guests
within," he added, lifting his pike with a shrug of apology.

"What does he say?" asked Edmund.

Ester could see that the Frankish language of this land

proved a challenge to the English knights. Even with her knowledge of the tongue spoken from Normandy to Champagne, Ester had difficulty. They had traveled as far as Burgundy, by Ester's guess, and she had trouble understanding this castle creature's dialect.

"This is a very small fortress," Ester told Edmund. She wanted to shield the young knight from disappointment. "Perhaps bargaining for entrance is not worth the trouble."

"He will welcome us in, won't he?" asked Edmund.

"Edmund, this manservant is afraid."

"Afraid!" responded Edmund, with something very like a good-humored laugh. "So are we, or we would not seek the shelter of this little tower."

"He is afraid of *us*," said Ester.

Of you she would not say.

"He will not let two ladies hide in his tower!" said Edmund in a tone of astonishment.

"I will not part from you, Sir Edmund," said Ester. "We are all one company."

Edmund searched his mind for some argument to this, but before he could speak again Ester said, "Upon my honor, Edmund, Ida and I will be at your side."

"No, we will be pleased to sit within walls," said Ida.

The guard was declaiming all the while on the nature of his responsibilities, to his lady, to her household goods, and to his lord's infants.

"There are children living here," said Ester, realizing at once the guard's reason for caution.

"Children," echoed Edmund thoughtfully.

"Six years old, and five years old, and one even younger," called the guard, seeing that word of small children had the desired effect on his supplicants. "A boy this high, and two girls."

"I see," said Edmund, who knew enough Frankish to understand that much. He turned his horse away.

"Pay this man," urged Ida. "He'll change his mind if he sees silver!"

"We mustn't let little ones," said Edmund without looking back, "have any part of battle."

Ester's leave-taking from her father weeks ago had been tearful, but joyful.

"Say a prayer for your mother," Bernard had said, embracing his daughter, "in the church of Santa Sabina." That famous church was the Roman sanctuary sacred to the name of women who had endured the pains of a difficult life.

"Where should I pay my thanksgiving," Ester had asked, "for your return to enjoying a healthy appetite for giblet pies and Rhine wine?" His complexion was ruddier than ever, and in a few days of vigor he had already put on weight.

"Before the same altar," her father had replied after a moment's consideration. "To Heaven's ear, I think, all prayers are the same."

The memory had all the more meaning now as she and Edmund departed from the shadow of the humble castle tower. Whether her friends were alive to see this day's sunset depended on the sheltering will of Heaven.

With the dust of their opponents growing ever closer, Ester put a hand on Edmund's reins. Surefoot responded at once, stopping his progress and cocking his ears.

"Arm us, Edmund," she said, "and let us fight beside you."

Like many court ladies, Ester had been schooled in the arts of hunting. She had rarely killed, but she could hit the target's center with a crossbow every time. She mentioned her skill, and made a pantomime, raising an invisible weapon to her shoulder.

"Can you indeed?" breathed Edmund in a tone of wonder and respect.

But before Wowen could retrieve the weapon from the tangle of baggage on the packhorse, the enemy arrived.

They were a throng of armored men, as Rannulf had reported, a fighting force that assembled in the clearing between vineyards opposite. The enemy knights rode the big, strong-boned mounts of war, and these animals were spiked with sweat and breathing heavily.

"Not a pretty assembly, are they?" said Ida, in a wan attempt at humor.

It was true that Ester had rarely seen such a travel-grimed, use-hardened gang of men. From gauntlet to buckle they were the stuff that peasant and lady alike beheld in nightmares.

"A parley, if you please," called Sir Jean.

❀ ❀ ❀

One of the battle group's squires, a lean-faced man, rode forward on a sweat-darkened bay.

As ignorant of war as Ester might be, she knew that a few minutes' delay would favor Sir Jean's men, allowing their horses to rest. But she was relieved when Nigel lifted a sword held hilt upward, a traditional symbol for peaceful intent, just as to hand a sword pommel first to an opponent was an earnest gesture of surrender.

Surely Saint George would not neglect them.

Even so, she felt the soft leather sack within her cloak, sensing the holy relics within. She could not prevent the feeling: She was afraid. Peasants sheltered behind oxcarts and the rich greenery of the rows of distant vineyards as Edmund and Wowen made their way toward the center of the clearing.

Ester's two companions rode horses well rested enough to show frisky curiosity in each other, and also in the as-yet unfamiliar animals across the road beyond. The dust-streaked fighting men along the edge of the vineyards bared their teeth in unpleasant smiles, and commented among themselves, their eyes on the two young ladies.

"Not so much as one pinch of kindness," said Ida, her voice trembling, "in the lot of them."

25

EDMUND DID NOT LIKE THE WORN FEATURES
of the enemy squire from the moment he opened his mouth.

"The worthy knight Sir Jean de Chartres," said the
squire, "extends his greetings to Sir Edmund Strongarm
and his fellows." The sunburned squire gave Edmund a
long and measuring look as he spoke.

Sir Jean, well behind his men, made no effort to settle a
helmet over his head, or to take up his shield, content to look
on as his charger shook its mane, still breathing hard. A
stream of cold water ran behind the small group of pilgrims,
the sound audible throughout the clearing. The thirsty
horses snorted and shivered with anticipation, nosing the air.

"Sir Edmund Strongarm," sang out Wowen, "greets Sir
Jean de Chartres, and his assembled knights."

Edmund felt a trickle of sweat run down his cheek. A
knight's helmet was a cumbersome object, and Edmund
doubted he would ever become used to wearing one. Every
sound from the outside world took on a sinister iron tenor.
He nudged Surefoot just a few paces closer.

A well-mannered squire or a herald usually began a

parley between fighting forces as the knights themselves remained largely silent. It was easier to undo an accidental insult delivered by a squire, and easier for a knight and his companions to measure an enemy while a functionary engaged in courtesies.

But Wowen, the sole squire available to perform this duty on behalf of the pilgrims, was a beginner. Edmund moved even closer, ready to press his mount forward if Wowen's courage failed—or if there was any further sign of danger.

"I am Hamo Peche, newly appointed squire to Sir Jean," the long-armed, wiry squire was saying, tugging at his tunic as he spoke. "I can offer a proposal that may spare the life of you, young squire, and your lords."

Wowen introduced himself in response, performing his duties well. The young squire replied in the formula known by any child who had ever played at combat—that Wowen's lord would be grateful for a way to show mercy to Hamo and his masters.

Hamo was a veteran of many fights, judging by the scars on his arms, and he was no longer young. He had been left behind by ill fortune, Edmund assumed, or because fever or drunkenness had rendered him unfit for a holy war. Such men were eager to prove themselves, the knight believed, and likely to hide a weapon in a legging or a sleeve.

Hamo's eloquence began to falter. "My master will kill you all," he said. "Prepare to bite the ground."

This was crude beyond belief. Wowen straightened in

his saddle. The youth recognized that he was dealing with a squire who knew little of good manners, or even decent speech. *Bite the ground* was a phrase from hardy drinking songs, unworthy of the occasion.

Sir Jean made an impatient motion in the distance, *Hurry up,* working his head into his iron helmet. The former Crusader could not entirely control his men or their thirsty animals. Sir Jean's men were calling out coarse jokes now, in yet another dialect Edmund did not understand. Edmund recognized them as *routiers*, men who traveled the roads to hire their war skills to any bidder. Too bereft of faith to respond to a Crusade, or too habitually disobedient to take part in a fighting force, they wore weather-tarnished riding armor, and carried light hunting lances, the better to run down fleeing footmen.

"My lords will not surrender so much as a chestnut," said Wowen.

In response to this, Hamo shot one lean hand up a sleeve and withdrew a long, blue-iron spearhead.

He thrust this shaftless weapon at Wowen. Only the quick reflexes of Wowen's mare, shying at the unexpected motion, kept the blade from plunging into the boy-squire's chest.

As it was, the ugly iron weapon caught Wowen's tunic, and when Hamo tried to withdraw the point it tangled there in the woolen fabric. Edmund recognized the weapon as the head of a throwing spear, a javelin. It was not uncommon for these items to be carried as daggers—they made effective stabbing blades.

The enemy squire wrestled the iron point free and struck again, a two-handed blow. This time Wowen was able to raise an arm and fend off the assault. The host of enemy knights raised a cheer at this sudden fighting, and in a ragged, rippling motion, the *routiers* began their attack.

Edmund drew his sword as a passing knight gave him a negligent thrust with a lance. Surefoot heard the whisper of blade leaving sheath, and prompted by Templar training, lunged forward, into Hamo's mount. One downward blow from Edmund's sword cut Hamo's arm through, and the squire tumbled from his saddle. The severed limb lay inert, like a thing that had never lived.

Edmund was shocked at the sight, and he pieced together the event that had just taken place—his heavy blade lifted high, the slaughterhouse crack of bone, the whisper of the leather armor shearing. The young knight had never struck such a single, telling blow with a broadsword, and in his emotional turmoil he had the instant, fleeting fantasy of seizing the severed arm and forcing it back into place.

Hamo sprawled, gleaming with scarlet, trying to drag the rest of his body toward the arm. Sir Jean, too, was taking a long moment to survey the grievous injury, and Edmund did something he regretted at once.

While the big Chartrian knight was distracted by the sight of the arm—surely the fingers weren't reaching, grasping—Edmund struck Sir Jean's helmet, a single, deep-cutting blow. Sir Jean fell to the ground with a cloud of dust and a Frankish curse, plainly more shaken than hurt.

Edmund took advantage of the momentary respite to turn in his saddle and call out for Ester, and for Hubert, worried that the *routiers* might well make short work of them.

There was no response.

With a throaty cheer the attackers surrounded the band of pilgrims, swords lifting and falling in the dusty afternoon sunlight.

At that moment Sir Jean struggled to his feet and issued some inaudible cry, gesturing, angry now, all protocol forgotten.

Sword to sword, the big knight was indicating with his gestures, throwing down his shield and hurrying toward Edmund's mount. A profound dent marred his helmet, and the Chartrian lifted a hand to his head for a moment. Then he reached out, pulled Wowen from his mare, and dragged the young squire like a boneless thing.

The knight called out a further challenge, gazing up at Edmund through the eye-slits of his headgear, holding the struggling squire in one mail-clad fist.

Edmund desired nothing but to ride to the defense of Ester and her companion, but the big knight shook the squire so hard that Wowen could make no sound. Then he threw the boy aside, and seized Edmund's leg. As big as Edmund was, the Chartrian was no small man, and he had the grip of a giant.

Edmund kicked, kicked again, feeling his weight shift as the big man's effort proved successful.

Sir Jean gave a further, desperate tug, and Edmund tumbled to the ground.

26

"FORM A HEDGEHOG," NIGEL SANG OUT AS the parley across the clearing collapsed. It was clear to Ester that this term referred to a purely defensive formation, shields up and swords bristling against the onslaught of the approaching knights. Hubert motioned meaningfully to her, *Keep your head down.*

And Ida whispered at her side, a ceaseless prayer repenting of all sins.

Rannulf was the first to leave this protective position, before the first lancer had struck. As the master knight took a stance, his sword arm cocked and his shield raised high, Ester felt everything grow cold. The sun, which had been a source of warmth until then, now cast an icy radiance.

Rannulf fended off the deliberately aimed lance with a blow of his shield, and drove the point of his blade into the barding—the leather covering—that protected the attacking knight's warhorse.

Until that moment, Ester had clung to the hope that the skirmish might be brief, a matter of a few threats and windy curses, to be concluded by a payment of silver. In Ester's experience at court, money salved all injury, and she believed that the threat of strife between knights was largely a form of extortion.

But the warrior confronting Rannulf responded with a series of thrusts, towering over Rannulf from his saddle and seeking gaps where the veteran knight's chain-mail coif left his flesh exposed. The horse gradually succumbed to his injury as this effort failed, collapsing to the ground. Rannulf set about killing the knight, blood gleaming on armor.

Hubert joined Rannulf, protecting the seasoned knight from an attack from his flank. The young knight was effective with his weapon, parrying and thrusting, driving off a new assailant, a man with a white plume flowing from his helmet.

Even in the confusion, however, it was clear that most of the attack's momentum was lost as horses hurried past the tangle of combat, and plunged their muzzles into the fast-running stream. Clydog defended the two ladies with a wood ax, lifting his voice in a battle lyric. Nigel left the last pretense of a purely defensive formation and went on the attack himself.

The silver-haired Nigel harried the improvised rear-guard of this confused mass, wounding men with fast sword work. Clydog successfully intimidated an approaching squire with his bellowed war verse, but soon the two ladies were exposed under the sifting rain of dust.

Ester saw it as it happened. An attacker—a shield bearer judging by his simple leather helmet—struck Clydog a stunning blow. The redoubtable retainer staggered, and sank to one knee. The scutifer—a muscular youth with dazzling blue eyes—threw aside his pike and seized Ida. The young man gave out a cry of possession that was nearly lost in the general roar of man and beast.

Ester worked with determined effort at the last knot holding the crossbow suspended with the baggage. Finally, she despaired of freeing the weapon and turned instead to the pike, gleaming in the dust.

She picked up the weapon, surprised at the weight of the long, iron-headed span. Ester had seen hunters readying their spears as the beaters drove an antlered stag into ambush. She had also seen the hunt master's knife finishing off the bleeding hind.

She thrust with the pike, intending a threat more than an assault. The inhuman weight of the implement, however, caused the point to enter the attacker's thigh with more power than she had anticipated, into the soldier's muscle. The young man released Ida, who had been struggling and screaming, and gaped at Ester like a gored bullock.

"The Devil take thee, lady," protested the fighter—*the Dele tae thee.*

Ester withdrew the weapon with some difficulty, but before the young fighter could counter Ester's attack, he was distracted by a new tumult.

Farmworkers approached, dressed in the beige wool tunics of their class, some fitting stones into their slings and others hurling stones with their naked hands, dozens of howling field hands. Men dressed in the dark gray, soft-combed wool of yeomen or farm steward's assistants also approached, bending bows.

As a rule, knights loathed and resented archers. While the crossbow was tolerated as a variety of *gyn*—war engine—employed by noblemen and their ladies, knights had no respect for the common bow and arrow. Ester looked on now as an arrow hissed through the air.

This force of laboring folk was led by a figure in a flowing blue hood and gown, and joined by the unshaven pikeman from the castle tower, the guard now hurrying into the clearing and calling out encouragement to the farmers.

Three children held a large, billowing banner at the top of the castle tower, and as Ester watched they managed to unfurl the heavy pennant. It bore a faded Agnus Dei—the Lamb of God.

The fighting broke into confusion, and scattered.

The lady approached Ester, taking her by the hand.

"By the grace of God," said this gentle-voiced woman—*Par la grace de Dieu*—"I am glad to see you unhurt." Her gown had been a rich blue, judging from the deep color still visible in the folds of the garment, but the cloth was faded now, and Ester recognized the needlework that had kept the sleeves in repair.

Ester prepared some high speech of her own, but a distant sound of violence dashed the words from her lips.

At the edge of the scarred and sodden clearing, Sir Edmund and Sir Jean were still fighting.

27

SIR JEAN WAS A BETTER SWORDSMAN THAN
Edmund—the younger knight could see that at once.

Edmund parried Sir Jean's violent attack, each blow a
shock to his joints and sinews. The youth was astonished at
the older knight's speed and craft, and Edmund now
regretted throwing aside his shield.

But he remembered a few elementary fighting lessons
of his own. The young knight kept his stance centered,
equal weight on both feet. He fought purely defensively at
the start, backing away and circling to the right, away from
the power of Jean's sword arm.

The afternoon sun was hot against Edmund's iron helmet, and the armor was heavy, chafing against his shoulders.
The helmet limited his visibility, too, and when one especially violent blow turned the iron bucket askew for an
instant, Edmund could see nothing at all until he raised a
mail-clad hand and readjusted it.

Through the heavy metal tub of his helmet, Edmund
made out the ebbing sounds of battle far across the clearing,
as what seemed to be a small army of vineyard laborers

made fast work of what was left of Sir Jean's men. The Chartrian was aware of this fading skirmish, too, and swung his weapon with increasing desperation.

Sir Jean slipped in a puddle of gore, and stepped right into the palm of his squire's severed limb, the lifeless fingers seeming to close around his boot.

Both knights stopped fighting.

Sir Jean lifted a hand, and called out a muffled, "One moment, I pray."

Kill him now.

Was it Wowen's voice, the young squire jumping up and down, well away from the skirmish? Or was it some violent sprite, or perhaps an urging from inside Edmund's own heart?

The big Chartrian knelt and lifted the severed arm, and placed it beside the now inert body of Hamo. This gesture of respect and compassion for a fellow fighter touched Edmund.

And it convinced the young knight that there had already been enough death under Heaven in recent months. Even when they began to fight again, Edmund bore the older man no ill will. The big Chartrian had been a fellow Crusader, after all, and a feeling of comradeship gave Edmund the incentive to close on Sir Jean once more, grappling hard this time, refusing to be thrown off.

28

EDMUND FELT THE OLDER KNIGHT GIVE way slightly, long minutes of effort beginning to tire the veteran.

"By the holy cross, Sir Jean," Edmund managed to say, in a tone both correct and heartfelt, "please sheathe your sword."

Perhaps there was a moment during which Sir Jean appreciated Edmund's suggestion. The moment did not last long. With a deft wrench and bob, like a market-day wrestler, the big knight escaped Edmund's grasp.

With a nimbleness surprising in such a weary swordsman, Sir Jean slipped among the pack animals, cutting one free, escaping with the startled, snorting steed into the vineyards. Only the occasional shaking of far-off vines, or the rising, startled flight of a crow, marked his passage.

"Fifty pennies," called Sir Nigel, arriving helmetless and red-faced with exertion, "for the head of Sir Jean."

The farmworkers brandished their implements, giving a cry of enthusiasm. This was a considerable bounty. The services of a war-proven knight could be purchased for ten pennies a day, a squire for less.

And the farmers, excited at having driven squires and shield bearers into the acres of tall, grape-laden vines, were keen at the prospect of running down an even more distinguished warrior. No knight liked to be forced to retreat, and Edmund felt a further degree of sympathy for the man.

Hubert pounded Edmund on the back, as Wowen helped free his head from the confines of the helmet. How refreshing the air was! And how sweet the sounds of crow-calls and horses sneezing. For a moment Edmund hoped he would never have to wear a helmet again.

"Another few strokes," said Hubert, his voice hoarse with relief, "and you'd have had him begging for quarter."

Edmund felt weak in every limb. He shook his head, thankful to be alive. "Another few blows, Hubert," said Edmund with a laugh, "and I would have fainted dead away."

Edmund was grateful at the light in Ester's eyes as she set the end of her pike—that was unmistakably what it was—on the ground, leaned on it like a castle guard, and asked, "Are you certain, Edmund, that you are not hurt?"

Edmund's response died on his lips.

He hurried to Ester, reaching out, but afraid to touch her and cause her further pain.

There was gore on her hand. And on her mantle, dark stains.

"This blood," she said, "is not my own."

"Ester, I thank God!" gasped Edmund, forgetting to call her *my lady* or *good Ester,* as courtesy decreed.

If Ester was in the least offended, she gave no sign.

The clash of steel against wood came from far across the vineyard, in the direction of Sir Jean's pursuers. The sound of cries of encouragement and pain, too, drifted through the dark green rows of vines.

At last the peasants limped back into the clearing, their homespun tunics sweat-darkened and torn.

One of the peasants fell to his knees, calling out in his dialect that the big knight had eluded them.

Nigel called for Rannulf, and gave a clipped command to Edmund.

They came across Sir Jean's mount dead at the far edge of the vineyard.

A crude flint-blade hatchet was buried in the animal's head. Both Surefoot and Strikefire bridled at the sight of the stricken animal, and it was not the first time Edmund felt as much pity for a horse as for a man.

They found Sir Jean up to his waist in the slow-moving current of a river. He was challenging his enemies through his helmet, but had not bothered to draw his sword again— a knight reserved his weapon for opponents he respected.

Peasants stood on the bank and showered the big

knight with missiles, sling stones, and smooth river stones, the projectiles dashing the slow current all around the knight. Archers took careful aim and loosed their shafts, and while the arrows glanced off the armor, they left punctures in the knight's coat.

"You are weak puppy dogs," bellowed the Chartrian. "You are little strengthless piglets," he called, his voice growing hoarse. An arrow had found its way under his mail coif, the armor protecting his throat, and protruded there, a yellow shaft.

Edmund called for the attack to cease, spurring his mount among the taunting, stone-throwing farmworkers. His English imperatives, *stoppe*, *ceese*, and *do way*, were lost among the howls and jeers of the attackers. No knight wanted to lose his life in a battle against a foe like this. Edmund worked to put his mount and his own body between the big Chartrian and his enemy peasants. The laboring folk simply scampered to new positions on the bank, singing out taunts.

Rannulf, after a long moment of looking on, shaking his helmeted head, used his lance to part the peasants, knocking them to the ground.

But it was too late.

Edmund's offered hand was lost on Sir Jean, the knight reeling, hands to his helmet as he staggered, struck by yet another arrow, and another jagged rock, missiles that glanced away but punished him nonetheless.

With a muffled sigh, the knight fell back and sank into the water.

❀ ❀ ❀

By the time Edmund hauled the big man out of the current—his former enemy's mail shirt catching on river reeds, his helmet dragging like an anvil—the knight was no longer breathing.

Edmund had once seen a priest shake an infant awake, a child who had toddled into a duck pond. Edmund tried to work the same miracle, but the Chartrian would not respond, his lips blue, his eyes unseeing.

Edmund managed a prayer for his soul, and Rannulf knelt to make the sign of the cross. It was considered prudent to express some kind remark about the departing spirit, to avoid bad luck, but all Edmund could manage was a thick-voiced, "Sir Jean was afraid of no man."

A burly peasant, his hands sticky with sap, stepped close, making a suggestive motion with a wood ax, asking for the slain knight's head. Rannulf pushed him away with one hand, but as he did, his fingers left red marks on the woodsman's tunic.

Blood streamed down from the knight's sword arm.

Sir Rannulf was hurt.

29

THE LADY OF THE CASTLE WAS ISOLDA DES Roches, a woman whose conversation Ester understood well enough, as long as they both spoke the stiff, courtly Frankish of envoys and noble travelers.

"My husband is off fighting to capture the Holy Sepulcher," said Isolda, in the tone of someone recounting a timeworn grief. "Every night I pray for his return." *Although some Crusaders have already begun to find their way home*, she did not have to add, *mine has not.*

The lady of the estate had managed the farmland, with the aid of a steward. All over Christendom such women were carrying on the responsibilities of harvest and repair, lifting prayers every evening for the safe return of husbands and fathers.

"And you are all," added the lady of the castle, arousing herself from her sadness, "bound for Rome?"

"By the grace of God," said Ester, "and with the merciful help of my lady Queen Eleanor."

This was far from the first time Ester had mentioned the queen in Isolda's presence. She was reminding the good

Lady Isolda that she had nearly allowed a party of pilgrims endowed by a royal lady to be killed or captured by the merest riffraff of knighthood.

Ester spared many long glances toward Rannulf. The legendary knight wore a white linen bandage around his right arm. An accidental cut from a halberd borne by an elderly sheepshearer had hurt the seasoned knight far worse, Ester believed, than Rannulf would admit. Even now, blood peppered the weave of the bandage.

The four English knights were enjoying various kinds of cheese pie—dishes unfamiliar to both Ester and her companions—accompanied by *flore frittours*—fried flowers, another unfamiliar delicacy. The pitchers of red and white wine were plentiful, but Ester detected that the wine had been heavily watered. Thick red wine was highly regarded medicine. This weak stuff, Ester knew, would do Rannulf little good.

Weak wine and a bit of pie crust were all Ester was able to swallow—food and drink held no pleasure for her just now. Edmund and Hubert, too, ate more sparingly than she would have expected. In addition to the demise of Sir Jean de Chartres, three other combatants had died that day. Hamo Peche was dead of his wounds, and two men had been slain by Rannulf: one Apollinaris de Quincy, and a highly honored warrior fallen on hard times, William Shortbeard. A local priest had promised that these knights would receive appropriate burial.

The remaining group of very much alive but sword-hacked squires and badly bruised shield bearers had been rounded up and locked in a granary by a limping Clydog and a gang of farmhands. The sturdy retainer had recovered from the blow to his head, but at the same time seemed diminished by it, slow of speech and weary.

The traditional ransom sought for these captured men would be a welcome source of income for the des Roches estate, and the captives accepted their lot as temporary prisoners with some grace. In all likelihood some needy baron would offer full price for the entire group.

The acts of violence Ester had witnessed that day were enough to make her uncomfortable with her companions. She had heard the queen herself say that when a man was killed before your eyes, you prayed for the peace of his soul, and put it all out of your mind with a song about the turtle-dove.

It was a philosophy Ester was trying to live up to, with only partial success. When she closed her eyes, she pictured blood-greasy swords, and she was amazed that she herself had been able to prick an enemy's flesh.

Amazed—and sickened.

"Is it true," Lady Isolda was inquiring, "that you will attempt to brave the Great Saint Bernard Pass?"

"It is the route pilgrim travelers usually take," said Ester, grateful to be distracted by conversation.

"It is," agreed Isolda, with troubling simplicity.

Guides from Savoy, the country near the great mountains of the Alps, usually brought travelers through the pass, aided by inns run by an order of monks dedicated to assisting wayfarers. The two-week trek was famous as a harrowing experience, and yet over the years merchants and government agents came and went, enduring the legendary hardships—and surviving.

"We will depart for the foothills tomorrow," said Ester, "if it please God."

"As challenging as the mountain trek has always been," said Isolda, dipping a fried blossom into olive oil, "it is all the more desperate now."

Rannulf made no effort to hide his indifference. He yawned.

"No combat is too challenging for Edmund Strongarm here," offered Hubert encouragingly.

Isolda responded with a pitying smile.

Ester decided that she was developing a particularly intense dislike for the lady of this castle. "Pray tell us," said Ester, keeping her tone sweet, "what you mean."

"The route is far too dangerous now for your small party," said Isolda with the air of someone with superior knowledge. "Bandit warriors hold the mountain pass. Many travelers have died up there on the ice."

"Do we appear weak?" responded Ester.

Isolda adopted a tone both more familiar and more respectful when she added, "The journey—it is too difficult, my lady, I fear."

"What foolish brigand-knights are these, my lady?" asked Nigel, lamplight in his eyes.

"I am warned that a young man of good name," answered Isolda, adopting a more formal tone in addressing the knight, "collects a toll from travelers. From those who cannot pay he collects their heads. He is the younger son of a landed family, and unlikely to inherit much." The plight of younger sons—who rarely inherited wealth—and their relative penury, was famous throughout Christendom.

"Who is this man-eating nobleman?" asked Nigel.

"He is called Conrad of Saxe," answered Isolda smoothly. "I understand he has a greedy army of iron-hats," she added, using the common phrase for hired soldiers.

Watching Isolda meet Nigel's lively gaze gave Ester an insight into her. It had been too long since the lord of Castle de Roches had sat at this table. Ester knew that, even in a noble soul, solitude breeds lust.

"You are gracious to warn us," said Ester.

Before they all retired for the night, the three wide-eyed children of the castle were led in by a timid house servant.

The children spoke well, made every show of high manners, and Ester was touched at the tenderness in the eyes of the knights as they tousled hair and bid the young ones sleep well.

Was this the same Sir Rannulf who had killed two men that very day, now wishing God's peace on the awestruck children?

And was this Edmund, who had cut off an arm, now laughing so sweetly?

It was a blessing, Ester felt, to sleep in a castle again, even a small *bastille* like this.

"Our knights fight well, and with good heart," Ida was

saying, mending a hem in her skirt by the quaking light of a candle stub. "But what will they do when frostbite seizes us in the mountain waste?"

"Heaven will defend us," said Ester, for a moment too tired to worry.

The welcome rustle of her bedding, a blanket stuffed with sweet straw, whispered at Ester's ear. When she closed her eyes she saw the bawling profile of a horse, and the flash of steel.

"The Alps," Ida was saying, expressing common knowledge, "harbor leagues of devils."

"Do you think, Ida," asked Ester sleepily, "that you yourself could use a sword?"

"No, by my faith. Never, dear Ester." Ida hesitated. "Except, I do believe, to save your life."

III
The Devil's Pathway

30

THE BAND OF PILGRIMS FIRST SAW THE
Alpine peaks a few days later.

Edmund had been riding in advance of the others,
upward along the increasingly sloping foothills, with the
three Savoyard guides immediately behind, each one taking turns telling endless anecdotes, to the disbelief and
mocking jollity of his mates. The guides disdained horseback and preferred to show their mettle by leaping from
one mossy rock to another.

Moss of every color and lichen of every hue splashed
rock and pebble, hairy, scabby, warty outgrowths of every
breed of furry vegetation, but the mountaineers never
slipped. Edmund envied them their sense of balance, and
hoped that Ester would not think less of him for not trying
to equal their ability.

No traveler loved mountains, or any other wasteland,
and the tales of pilgrims losing toes to frostbite and eyesight
to snow blindness were the stuff of legend. For some days
now the unmistakable lift of the land had promised thinner
and thinner air. The horses had labored at times, and the

streams were fierce, rushing water nearly too cold to drink.

The villages they had passed had been tiny hamlets, peaked roofs cloaked with grasses, and the nanny goats were long-haired, a breed apparently suited to the increasing slopes of the hills all around, green fields that rose up toward the noon sun, scored by generations of nimble-footed herds. Innkeepers of wood-clad, high-timbered inns had hosted them with special deference, recognizing them as pilgrims, and more than one had offered them each an extra birchwood cup of beer at no additional cost, as a gesture of condolence—or even pity—for folk about to endure the hardships of the Great Saint Bernard Pass.

But for all the turns and switchbacks of the ever-climbing trail, Edmund had not seen the peaks themselves. Every viewpoint was a mass of cloud, towering curds of weather. Even when the time came, when they looked down into a valley veiled with a rainbow, and the increasing altitude ached in the lungs, Edmund had not seen the mountains plain, naked, and white as he had heard them to be.

In truth, Edmund had gradually reassured his uneasy mind that when he saw the famous Alps, he would feel a rush of relief at how gentle and wind-rounded they turned out to be.

Hubert had agreed. "There won't be any mountains at all," he said with a wink. "They are the stuff of stories."

And then the time came.

A frog splashed in a flower-choked pond—it was strange how frogs endured the chilly, late summer nights only to sport in the bright sun. A fly—one of those that attack the eyes of horses—descended on Edmund and he swatted it away. The bell of a goat or sheep sounded somewhere.

Surefoot rounded a hillside.

And Edmund was confronted by the high, snow-scarred mountains.

The air was cold.

A waterfall stitched downward across the shadows, too far away to make a sound, and a bird of prey circled, fighting for altitude, in a vale far downslope from where Edmund found himself gripping the reins.

The young knight climbed down from Surefoot, half falling, and leaned against the horse for support.

"Yes, those intimidating peaks are your first glimpse of the Alps, Sir Edmund, what did you expect?" said the Savoyard guide—or some such remark.

"We're climbing into *those*?" Edmund allowed himself to ask, breathless with more than altitude.

"Until you walk on bleeding stumps," said the guide with a laugh, indicating Edmund's feet.

The guide may not have expressed quite that message. No one could really understand their dialect. They conversed in a patois so individual to each village that the mountaineers themselves could very nearly not understand one another. Hubert and Edmund had made a game of mock translations of the Savoyard tongue, and Edmund had the feeling that their half-comic translations were inadvertently close to accurate.

The guides wore tasseled woven wool caps and high wool leggings, all the way above their knees. "Come along, poor fools," laughed one of the guides, in Edmund's mental, half-serious translation. "We're marching you to your deaths."

"There must be a way around those peaks," protested Hubert, likewise climbing from his mount.

The guides laughed and whistled in response, three of the merriest men Edmund had ever known. "Freeze your bones on the ice, pilgrims!" the lead guide seemed to say, cracking a leather strap he used as a whip. He waved them all forward with a laugh, and added something like, "Die, travelers, up there where no one will find you."

The truth was that these hearty climbers often stretched out a supporting hand, and found the sweetest springs of water and thickest patches of grass for the horses. Edmund had a high regard for them, and was grateful for their rough cheerfulness.

"I fear these happy mountaineers, Ester," joked Edmund when the young woman joined them, letting her horse feed on the fine yellow flowers of the trailside. In truth, despite his apprehensions, Edmund would rather be nowhere else right then.

"I believe they must be the sons of mountain goats," offered Ester.

"Or their fathers."

The young lady laughed.

❊ ❊ ❊

When Rannulf and Nigel came up the trail, however, Edmund felt a renewed stab of concern.

Rannulf's features were shadowy, and he did not use his right arm, employing his left hand to hold the reins. Nigel rode close behind his old friend, and several times during the trip up the foothills the two knights had conferred privately.

Rannulf and Nigel paused side by side on the trail now, leaning back in their saddles to take in the sight of the peaks as Edmund joined them.

"It will snow tonight," said Rannulf.

Strikefire nuzzled Surefoot to one side, skirmishing over a tuft of wildflowers. Surefoot gave a playful bite in response, but moved. As the sun eased behind a shard of rock, Edmund saw the vapor of his own laugh in the sudden, profound shadow.

"Does Rannulf ride easy?" Edmund asked Nigel, as though Rannulf could not overhear. It was a polite way to frame the question, and it was also safely worded. A direct question about one's health could reach a devil's ear, and cause bad luck. Here in the mountains a knight could not be too careful.

"Rannulf is more oak tree than man," said Nigel. "Isn't that right, old friend?"

Rannulf himself sighed, as though impatient—or embarrassed. Or perhaps some darker, more secret intent made him look away.

Nigel reached down to straighten Strikefire's rein

chains—a link had become tangled. The charger exhaled a gush of air, shying away, and Nigel offered a gentle *cluck-cluck*. "It's all twisted," he said. *To-wrast.* Nigel laughed softly, and gave the horse a soothing pat, reassuring both mount and man.

But *to-wrast* meant more than "twisted," Edmund knew. It also could mean "amiss." And Edmund found himself that night, lying on a hard pallet in a smoky, naked-timbered inn, thinking: amiss.

Our efforts are all amiss, and Nigel knows it.

31

EDMUND RECOGNIZED THE HUSH THAT
descended around the inn the following morning.

Rannulf had been wise in foreseeing the weather. The
morning was cold and quiet. The young knight crawled
from under the bristly wool of the blanket, convinced that
no monk ever wore a hair shirt more prickly than the blankets of this high country.

He found Sir Nigel in the doorway, watching snow
swirl down from the sky in the very early morning. The
snow was serene, and it was familiar. Edmund had loved
the long snowy mornings of his early boyhood, helping his
father plane barrel staves. He had heard that some of these
mountain wastes were snow-clad year-round, and now he
believed it.

"He can ride," said Nigel, answering Edmund's unspoken question and taking a swallow of his usual morning
beverage, warm wine.

Edmund could not suppress a very slight sigh of impatience. The journey to the Holy Land had softened some
toughness in Nigel's character, and made him more given

to laughter. But sometimes he still retreated to the terse manner of old, a warrior who would rather strike a blow than talk.

Sir Nigel stirred, perhaps suddenly aware of having offended the younger knight. "Edmund, Rannulf will not speak of his hurt."

The trail was always in shadow now, except when the meager path snaked upward, over a ridge, and then sunlight was near-blinding off the snowmelt.

Rude huts had been fitted together beside the trail, peaked structures of rough-barked timbers, commanded by a crucifix or a figure of Our Lady. And more than once these shrinelike shelters were overlooked by the key-carrying image of Saint Peter. Travelers associated the venerable saint with stone, and there was rock all around, devout mounds of it.

One afternoon Edmund repaired a shrine that had been desecrated, chopped with an ax, the holy image removed. Edmund put a handful of late-season flowers on the simple wooden shelf that served as an altar, and prayed to Saint Mark, who was God's lion and a source of courage. Wowen joined in, the young squire saying, "Don't worry, Sir Edmund, we won't let the Devil's harm go unmended."

The first travelers' hospice, when they attained it—a barnlike building of dark wood, surrounded by glittering stony rubble—was empty. An order of monks was celebrated for their ministry to travelers, but within the expansive hall of the shelter were only a few hacked pieces of broken furniture, and signs of darkened blood on the stone-slab floor.

The Savoyards consulted with one another, hitching their belts and pointing upward, toward the mountain heights. Now Edmund's all-but-imaginary grasp of their language become helpful.

"*Briganti* have done all this," they said, their usual spirits now thoroughly dampened. "*Banditti,* deaf to God."

"Is this the work of Conrad of Saxe?" asked Edmund.

One Savoyard crossed himself, and the others grew tight-lipped.

Nigel fell the next morning, fording a rushing stream, the roar of the water echoing so that no voice could be heard.

The surrounding peaks were covered in what the folk of Edmund's childhood called *myst-hakel*—a cloak of mist. Edmund had found himself singing earlier that day, the pretty tune with the chorus "and serue the God of Christen men." His hearing was poor with the thunder of white water, but he was certain Ester and Hubert joined in.

The travelers had left the tall, deep-rooted trees far behind. The last bushes, wind-knotted shrubs, gorselike greenery, had been left behind, too. The only fodder for the mounts was the scattered hay and summer grasses abandoned by monks in their apparent flight.

Nigel was in the lead, hooded and cloaked. Without warning, his horse went down, and then was up in an instant, like a thing that had not really happened. But the saddle was empty, and Nigel was nowhere to be seen.

Edmund plunged up to his knees in the numbing water, the hard current nearly cutting his feet out from under him. He groped for Nigel, and found the heavy fabric of his mantle with his fingertips. The young knight heaved the master warrior out of the all-but-freezing cascade.

"I am not hurt!" protested Nigel.

Rannulf looked down from the saddle, with a skeptical smile on his scarred features.

"No bones are broken," insisted Nigel, "by Heaven's mercy." The drenched and shivering knight stepped to Strikefire's bridle, and gripped it. "I am not," he said, breathing hard, " even so much as bruised." He considered, and then confided to his friend, "It's nothing one of my old pleasure wenches couldn't cure with a kiss."

When Clydog offered Nigel a blanket, however, the knight was pleased to throw it over his shoulder.

That evening as they approached yet another abandoned refuge, the simple building a silent hulk, Rannulf made a low *tssk-tssk* to his mount, and investigated a huddled, wasted heap of what resembled kindling and rags up the wind-stripped slope.

"The piteous wight," exclaimed Rannulf, when he returned, with uncharacteristic compassion. "A monk, I judge by his habit."

"How killed?" asked Nigel, who, like his old friend, took comfort in the hard facts of weaponry.

Rannulf made a motion, his finger across his throat.

It was not the first time Edmund felt a jolt of impatience with the master knight. Such a crude gesture could only offend and frighten the ladies.

32

ESTER LOVED THE STARS, SO CLOSE SHE WAS
sure that if she stretched her hand, the tiny chips of light
would part, quaking, and her hand reach through into
Heuenriche—the Kingdom of Heaven.

She loved hearing Edmund reassure Hubert that they
would all see him safely with Galena again, at peace within
the Roman walls. She was delighted at the way Edmund and
his friend made gentle mockery of the guides. She enjoyed
Edmund's songs, and his way of stopping to gaze with
wonder at a cloud formation or a glint of rain far below.

She and Edmund exchanged examples of lore—he
knew all there was to tell, it seemed, about wood elves and
enchanted pools of water. She was able to enlighten him
with more courtly legends, like the story of the pelican who
nourished her young on blood she pecked from her own
breast.

Rannulf was the only traveler who could gaze long into
the void. Pebbles knocked loose from the trail bounded and
echoed downward for several heartbeats. Horses snorted
and bridled, and Edmund calmed them with a touch.

"Perhaps you are descended from the centaurs," Ester said one morning, as Edmund heaved the heavy saddle blanket over his mount.

She meant it as an artful compliment, but Edmund gave an uncertain smile. "My family were English freedmen," he replied. He thought for a moment. "Who are these centaurs you mention?"

"The centaurs were half horse," she said, holding Surefoot's bridle.

"These horse-men live beyond the Great Sea, perhaps," said Edmund thoughtfully.

"They are creatures of legend," said Ester, "from long ago."

"I am half horse, though, even so," said Edmund. "And I think some animals are half human."

Why, she wondered, did he have to take every statement so seriously? While Hubert could banter with Edmund, and easily make the tall young knight break into laughter, Edmund treated Ester with a gentle deference.

One evening as Clydog was starting the cooking fire—blowing on an ember he carried wrapped in dry moss and a cunning nest of woven grasses—Rannulf offered Ester a blanket to sit on, freshly brushed by his own hand. The bearded knight did this without speaking, in his customary silence.

Edmund shook out a blanket of his own, and said, "Sir Rannulf, forgive me for saying so, but the Lady Ester deserves higher courtesy."

Rannulf stared at Edmund, saying nothing.

"Your manner is so austere," Edmund explained, exasperation in his voice. *Hausterne*. The word meant "rugged," but it also meant "harsh." "A lady is not an ox."

Edmund's tone was earnest to the point of confrontation, and Hubert and Nigel stood still, their features uneasy at hearing the legendary knight so bluntly criticized.

"Good Edmund, I am honored by Sir Rannulf's care for me," said Ester quickly and quite sincerely.

Rannulf let his shoulders rise and fall in a sigh. The seasoned knight had been aware of the glances between Edmund and the Lady Ester.

"I have few graces," Rannulf said after a silence, speaking with the self-conscious effort he would have used on a Latin verse. "But by God's wounds, Edmund and my lady, I apologize to all for any offense."

Devoid of self-pity as he was, Rannulf nevertheless required a vigil in the quiet, star-riddled dark to regain his usual detachment.

Walking alone at night was often fatal, even in England, where ponds and ditches claimed the lives of infants, drunks, and wayward sentries. In this wild land, to wander would mean to risk stumbling into an abyss. It was true, however, that Rannulf had a growing admiration for the manly Creator who could make such perilous summits, such cold, baleful wind, and such relentless torrents.

He stood a quiet, lone vigil, and relished the silence. Besides, alone under the starlight, he could unbind his wound and test the strength of his right arm. No corruption simmered in the ugly gash at the crook of his sword arm—Rannulf was grateful for that. But when he gripped the pommel of his sword, he could feel both pain and weakness in his muscles. A sinew had been cut, and it was not healing quickly.

Rannulf's mother had died giving birth to her son nearly forty summers ago. His father had been a castle steward, gifted at directing mortar work, erecting walls and towers for lords along the English coast. Albert of Rye had had enough silver to hire the best fighting instructors for the youthful Rannulf.

Rannulf was already a squire, serving a succession of battle-hungry warriors, when word came that a drunken knight had killed Albert in an accident, mistaking the honest castle man for one of his servants. Rannulf wasted no time in finding the wine-bloated knight, challenging him to a joust, and killing him.

But the ease of this revenge had stirred a hunger for more of the same in Rannulf, and his career had been a long string of killings carried out without much effort and surely without joy. Heaven for Rannulf would be carrying the prize of the drunken knight's head into his father's chamber day after day, and hearing his father gasp, "Who killed that wine-blind murderer?"

And then realizing the truth.

Yes, Father—it was me.

Now footsteps crunched toward Rannulf across the snow.

Instinct made the veteran knight reach for the sword at his belt. He winced at the pain in his limb. Then he recognized Edmund's tall form against the starlight.

"Please forgive me, Rannulf," said Edmund after a silence, "for speaking to you so churlishly."

There was something about Edmund that reminded Rannulf of his own slain father—a steadiness, and a gentle humor combined with good sense. Rannulf rarely indulged in introspection. The killer of so many men did not dwell on nightmares, nagging doubts, or his own past sins.

Rannulf gave what he could of a smile though his scarred lips, and nodded. He felt an inner tension vanish. "Give it not another thought," he said, warm with affection for the young man.

Most men found much pleasure in women, but Rannulf was not one of them. Nor did he favor the touch of men, beyond the simple and soul-strengthening embraces of companionship. Something in Rannulf's heart stood off from people altogether, but he counted himself a loyal friend.

"You are feeling strong again?" asked Edmund, laying a tentative, gloved hand on Rannulf's shoulder.

The veteran knight lifted his sword arm over his head, gripping an imaginary weapon, showing how he could raise it high.

He let his arm fall.

If only it were true, thought Rannulf.

The man killer did not admire deceit, and yet something kept him from voicing the truth. Indeed, to his own dismay he heard his mouth give out a lie—not that he believed it was a fact, but that he wished it so.

"It has knitted well," said Rannulf, carefully through his scarred lips, "and I am sound."

The horses stirred, and one of the mountain guides gave a low whistle of caution. In the pass ahead some sound, an ax fall or a dislodged stone, resounded.

The moment passed, and the horses grew quiet again, but both knights were joined with a single, uneasy thought.

They were being watched.

33

ESTER WAS THE FIRST TO SEE IT—A STUBBY tower of stone above the trail.

The structure was so far above them that the pilgrims had to shield their eyes to observe it in detail. A pile of stones near the squat edifice and the unfinished, irregular outline of a wall were evidence enough to prompt Edmund to observe, "It's newly thrown together, and falling down about as fast as they can pile it up."

"It's the usual Saxon work," Nigel said. "Square and clumsy."

"Where are these flesh-eating brigands?" asked Ida—timorously, but with a degree of spirit, too.

Ester was relieved when the first outlaw showed himself moments later, a long-legged man in a hood and a thick sheepskin kyrtle—a knee-length coat.

Her relief was real enough. Like Ida, she had been imagining cave-ogres bristling with battle axes and fork-headed pikes. This individual looked like a carter, or a mason's assistant—not a stupid sort, necessarily, but a man used to following instructions.

A second highwayman dropped down onto the trail ahead, a much shorter man, likewise well-padded with clothing. Both carried bows—battle-stained specimens, as far as Ester could make out. Each man sported a quiver, with a few white, goose-feathered arrows.

"The robbers have not put on much fat," said Ida, "by stealing from the monks' pantries."

It was true that the men accosting the pilgrims had a sunken look. The taller brigand said something to the lead mountaineer, but the Savoyards did not respond, retaining in their silence a certain proud reserve.

Hubert and Edmund loosened the swords in their scabbards, and Rannulf let his horse feel its way downslope a few lengths so that he could watch what took place from an angle. Ester was proud of the studied calm of her knights, especially of the easy way Edmund stroked Surefoot affectionately, with no sign of anxiety.

Ester reined in her mount and let Clydog and his packhorses draw up to her. She reached out and touched the chief retainer's shoulder.

The servant gave a start, and then a quiet, embarrassed laugh. The venerable servant had long since recovered from his battle injury, but like every one of the pilgrims, he had been altered by recent experience. He was leaner, sun-blistered, and he was quicker to offer praise to his companions.

Ester made a signal, acting out the cocking of a crossbow.

Clydog needed no further instructions, but as always the cordage binding the weapons and blankets was heavily knotted.

The criminals on the trail ahead may have heard the metallic noise the crossbow made as Clydog prepared the weapon. Certainly Nigel did, straightening in his saddle without stopping his cheerful flow of Frankish. The veteran knight spoke all the more loudly, expounding on their destination, and the subsequent holy places in Rome, so that the gangling criminal relaxed somewhat, and slipped the hood off his head. He made his way back along the line of travelers, assessing them. He eyed stirrups, leggings, belt buckles—items of value—and was growing pleased at his prospects.

But not as pleased as the outlaw would have been if he had guessed the truth. Travelers all adopted the same long-sleeved mantle and hood, and while some of the wool fabric was soft-combed, it was difficult to determine at a glance that this band of pilgrims included young women from a queen's court, each worth a healthy ransom.

This swaggering, long-boned brigand would not have been so self-assured unless he had reinforcements waiting, Ester knew, and she saw them at last, creeping up the gravel-strewn slope below. Perhaps a dozen spidery men approached on the downslope, and another two or three perched up above, rising and shielding their eyes against the sunlight.

Another joined them high above, the only man carrying a sword. This nobleman's flowing coat had been scarlet, and now was faded to a pale rose-colored pink. His chainmail sleeves were rust brown in the sunlight. To her surprise, the far-off aristocrat looked youthful, his fair hair blowing in the easy wind as he watched from the vicinity of his half-built tower.

"Conrad of Saxe looks as hungry as the rest," offered Ida quietly.

Indeed he did. And yet Queen Eleanor had often said that hunger gives the coward a hero's heart.

Ester leveled her crossbow at the brigand before her.

He was four or five strides away—sure to be a lethal distance—and he remained right where he was, glancing uphill toward his master for advice. But the nobleman was too far away to do more than strain his vision, both hands held against the sun.

Then the tall robber opened his scurvy-spotted mouth in a surprised smile as he met Ester's gaze. She could read his thought. *A woman.*

And at once his eyes narrowed. *But what sort of woman?*

The man was right in wagering his life on the likely assumption that Ester was a merchant's wife, or even a nun, able to hold a weapon but without the knowledge or the will to use it. Most crossbows required a strong pull of the firing latch, and were difficult to aim and release at once, without some experience. He was assuming that Ester did not know how to employ the weapon.

The blue-eyed brigand paused before Ester, and put a hand out to the hem of her mantle. It was a wool of quality— Ester had applied her own needle to the hem when it had needed repair. The man's weather-chapped fingers tested the virtue of the fabric with the care of a mercer, and he turned and bawled something down the slope of glittering gravel, a phrase in the Saxon tongue that Ester could understand easily enough.

"There is a lady."

The message echoed off the cliffs.

At the same time the robber announced this, he realized the implications regarding his own safety. The brigand backed away from Ester, nearly slipping and stumbling from the trail, and as he took his faltering, backward steps, he put out a hand to seize the bridle of Ida's palfrey, a smile barely masking his anxiety.

Courtly ladies often knew how to hunt, and, judging by his frightened expression, the brigand remembered this fact. Ester mustered what she could of the Saxon language, and said, "Do not lay a hand on her."

"*Hwat?*" gasped the long-legged man. He was either startled that Ester could manage a few words, or mystified by her accent. "My lady," he exclaimed with a laugh, "we will not hurt you." He said this even as his hand fumbled for and found Ida's foot in its stirrup.

Ida struggled, but his grasp was firm. He looked up at his prize, and without turning aside called out to his companions, "There are two ladies!"

Ester aimed and fired the crossbow in one easy movement. The long-limbed man released Ida's foot, brushing at the rough-spun cloth of his front like a man absentmindedly annoyed by a wasp.

The foreign object marring the front of his kyrtle was not an insect, however, but the protruding shaft of the quarrel. His fellow brigands called out, and the nobleman still far above on the rocky slope shouted a question that echoed and reechoed off the mountains.

"My lady," said the wounded man, his voice laden with apology as he lifted his hand to execute a shaky sign of the cross. He sank to his knees, and then melted farther. He stretched out unmoving, his eyes wide.

The Savoyard guides called out, leaping into action, waving their arms in an urgent, *Hurry! Hurry!*

Ride hard.

Ester wanted to cry out for her fellow pilgrims to wait—she had to offer a prayer for the mortally wounded man's soul.

34

"DO YOU THINK, ESTER," ASKED IDA, "THAT it was necessary? To kill the man?"

Ester had no ready answer. She observed Edmund's figure outlined against a snowbank, hands on his hips as he listened to the animated conversation of one of the guides. The Saxon tower, and the small army of brigands, was behind a high reach of cliff. Nigel and Rannulf had selected this site as a pilgrim camp—large, chalk-white boulders would make it easy to defend, even though it was not far from the outlaw fortification.

It was plain that the knights were eager for a fight. Hubert handed Rannulf a whetstone, Nigel pointing out the best place to stake the horses, all with very little speech but an alert companionship. Clydog blew on a fuming snatch of moss, and fire began to work against the gathering darkness.

Ester had no answer to Ida's questions.

"Now we can't negotiate with the brigands," Ida said, flinging down a blanket to cover the stony earth. "They'll want to chop us into suet."

Rannulf poured both of them a cup of shocking-cold

water from a leather jug. He had pulled the crossbow quarrel from the brigand's ribs—the wood-and-iron bolt was a precious object so far from a skilled armorer. His fingers were still sticky with blood.

Rannulf gave a quiet laugh, seeing Ester's troubled gaze. "Your act was a boon, my lady," he said. "Now we can fight."

A boon—a thing to be desired, nearly a blessing. That was how these men viewed unshriven death, Ester thought bleakly, so far from priest or chapel.

Ester could not share this outlook. She begged Heaven's mercy for the sin of causing a human death.

Ida put her hand on Ester's. "It's quite true, Ester," she admitted at last, "that I did not enjoy his scabby hand feeling my foot."

Ester had spent long evenings sitting with her father, the wick in the candle smoking and hissing, as the scholar leafed through priceless books of legends, stories of emperors in far-off countries, wise men who studied the triangle and the spleen, voyagers who encountered one-eyed giants.

One of Ester's favorite legends was the story of Hannibal the Great, a general from the ancient country of Carthage, who devised a way of marching elephants over these same Alps, so that he might do battle with the ancient Romans. Ester recalled, too, a ploy the famous general from Carthage had used to deceive an enemy shadowing him, perhaps here in this very same Alpine pass.

"The great general lit many cooking fires," Ester recounted to her friends, "and his enemy was confused into thinking he had been joined by reinforcements."

"That would be a cunning deceit!" exclaimed Sir Nigel, running a thumb along the blade of a dagger. "Conrad will think some band of stalwart monks, or even knights, has butchered and roasted a horse with us, and swelled our ranks by a score."

If Ester had felt superior to any knight at any time during her life, especially a storied killer like Rannulf, she felt chastened, and shocked into a more modest view of her own virtues, now that she had taken a life herself. At the same time she heard the voice of Queen Eleanor chiding her, *Be of good heart. And sing of the turtledove.*

They had to break up a half-ruined shrine for fuel. Soon it looked like a camp of forty travelers. The heat from the flames shivered the stars.

Ester did not want Edmund to depart from this firelight, but she knew Nigel's military enthusiasm paralleled that of Hannibal the Great. "While the enemy stalks closer, too afraid to attack," Nigel counseled, "we'll send a force up and around their flank. What think you, Rannulf? Will you climb the slope to trade blows with a few brigands?"

This last question was good-natured but challenging.

Rannulf bowed his head.

None of his companions spoke, the fire snapping and spitting.

"My love for my companions," confessed Rannulf at last, "is stronger than my sword arm."

Nigel gave a nod, as though to say, I guessed as much.

Before he set forth, Edmund found a moment alone with Ester.

She cradled the crossbow, at the very edge of the firelight. Wowen and the young servants were shifting back and forth throughout the now sprawling camp, trying to sound like a crowd of men, banging cooking pots, singing.

"Where is your mail shirt?" she asked.

Edmund arranged his mantle, and adjusted his belt. "It makes a climber feel clumsy," he said. "Or so the guides advise, if I understand them."

"But you'll carry your shield," she prompted.

"They say," said Edmund, choosing his words with care, "that a loving heart can suffer no wound."

The young lady, trained to speak artful phrases, could muster no response.

"If that is true, Ester," said Edmund, "then no blade can touch me."

35

EDMUND AND HUBERT CLIMBED THE STEEP
incline in the starlight.

Edmund climbed with as much faith in the enterprise
as he could gather, but he kept turning to look back. He
was worried about his friends.

The Savoyard guides had continued to impress
Edmund. While not warriors, the mountaineers had
showed stamina and pluck, and now they had supplied the
two young knights with a length of rope, gesturing that the
two might secure the cordage around each other's waists.

It probably would have been a good plan, if only they
had experience and ability enough to put it into effect. As it
was, Edmund carried the coil of hempen rope over his
shoulder—he thought it might provide some protection
against a sword.

Too high.

They were far too high above the campfires, the pin-
pricks of light far below. One further glance and Hubert
whispered, "Edmund, don't look down." *Dunna loke dun.*

They followed a goat path, or perhaps a trail worn into the naked ground by hell-inspired devils. Edmund's sword was an awkward weight, half tripping him, dragging on the rock's weathered surface. As the young knight found yet another foothold, pulling himself higher, he prayed that Saint John the Baptist, who had lived on flies and honeycomb in the wilderness, might give them strength.

It was colder up here, the path ahead a mere ghost across the gravel. There was no sign of Conrad. Edmund shivered, breathing into his hands. He felt breathless, and his lungs ached.

Hubert touched his arm.

A shadow was leaning against the moon-pale concretion of stone, the half-built tower. This particular shape was human, and wore a sword.

The camp far below did indeed look like the gathering of a few dozen folk, fires dancing, and Clydog made a great show of singing, some drinking song about a cat in love with a cow. His voice echoed and reechoed as Edmund's feet slipped silently across the snow.

Conrad folded his arms, his head to one side as though the merry, ribald music woke some longing in him. Nigel was joining in now, the verses rising upward into the night, a fine old song about a frog swelling to the size of an ox.

The brigand chief did not hear their approach. Edmund slipped, caught himself, inching forward. His fingertips were numb. Their enemy was a stone's-throw away.

If only my steps did not slip so, thought Edmund, or make such a leaden *crunch, crunch*.

But their adversary still did not hear them, drinking from a wineskin, and then drinking again.

Edmund put his finger to his lips, and Hubert gave an impatient nod.

But then Conrad drew his sword.

"Yield yourself into our hands," said Edmund, closing the gap in a few bounds, "and by Jesu we'll do you no harm."

Or this is what he tried to say. His words were thin at this altitude, and he felt dizzy. Starlight gleamed on Conrad's smile. The outlaw knelt, picked up a flat, ax-head-sized stone, and skimmed it easily through the air. The rock struck Hubert in the face.

The young knight fell, scrambling and struggling, trying to keep his body from pinwheeling down the rocky incline. He failed. Rocks chimed and clashed, tumbling downslope after him.

This was followed by a wind-marred silence. Edmund cried out his friend's name, and there was no response.

Conrad cut at Edmund as the young knight approached, a nearly accurate strike.

The noble brigand fought hard. Conrad's attack was so heavy that Edmund steadied his blade with his gloved left hand at times, closing his fingers around the steel and holding his weapon crosswise. Conrad fought very much like a nobleman's son, the moonlight in his golden hair. Edmund parried and countered like a fledgling knight, soon to fall before superior craft.

At last Edmund found solid footing, and thrust hard with his weapon.

The assault caught Conrad by surprise. Edmund tried another, even more well-aimed thrust, and found bone, just above the nobleman's knee.

Conrad turned and ran, with a loping, off-rhythm gait. He tried to climb the half-built steps to his tower, but the stones tumbled and slipped, unmortared and poorly set. The outlaw fled across the mountainside, and Edmund followed, the thin air burning his lungs.

He was able to pursue the outlaw, matching him stride for stride across the silver expanse of ice, until not far ahead the young nobleman stopped, his arms wheeling, fighting for balance.

The nobleman wavered, his ashen face looking back, his lips parted.

And then he vanished.

Edmund fell to his knees and crept forward.

An icy wind exhaled upward out of a cavernous emptiness, and even before he peered over the ledge, Edmund knew what he would see.

So what he actually beheld surprised him.

On a shelf of rocks, not far below, Conrad of Saxe was stirring, searching his body with tentative hands. The drop had not been far, and the nobleman rose to one knee, looking around at the deep blue moonlight reflected from the snow.

Steps approached, and Edmund gripped his sword.

"These Saxon brigands cannot fight," said Hubert,

breathing hard, blood streaming from his nose.

Edmund uncoiled the rope from around his arm. The cordage was hacked in places, but the rope was entire for the most part. He threw a length down to Conrad, who backed away from it as from a viper.

36

EVEN WHEN THE MANY CAMPFIRES EBBED, fuel spent, the wind swept the embers in slow, crazy spirals.

Yet another white-feathered arrow hummed through the dark, an angry, vicious sound, and Ester gathered her cloak more tightly around her. Another arrow struck the drowsy coals with an explosion of sparks, and somewhere beyond the camp a Saxon voice was lifted in a blaspheming taunt.

"The archer sounds tired," said Ida.

"And young," added Ester.

"They'll be out of arrows soon, my ladies," said Rannulf.

He stood near them, to shield the two from the metal-tipped shafts.

Clydog and his helpers joined Wowen in making a show of noise, laughing, shouting, splitting wood, as though a congregation of pilgrims populated the camp. "The Gib Cat in Love with His Lady Cow" was one of Queen Eleanor's favorite tunes. Bernard used to sing the ballad of the frog and the ox, so Ester was able to join in singing, too, as Rannulf and Nigel patrolled the perimeter of the camp on horseback, firelight glinting off their armor.

Eventually, Clydog chanted songs only he could remember. These were battle songs, obscure but thrilling verses, ballads of slain ranks of enemies, and of heroic ghosts rising up to join their living companions.

"Sing that one again, Clydog," Ester said. "The one about the young man no steel could wound."

The brigands commenced a probing assault well before dawn, but Rannulf's horsemanship was equal to running them down, sending them hoof-scored and scrambling. A further skirmish near the horses would have succeeded in cutting mounts free, except that Ida and Ester called out like furies, and joined in driving back the attackers.

Once during the night Ester was nearly certain that she heard the sound of swords clashing from somewhere very high in the mountain darkness. Surely not, she prayed. Surely Edmund had not climbed so far.

Ester saw Conrad of Saxe before she could make out either Hubert or Edmund, the nobleman finding his way down the trail with a curious stride.

It was a slow process, seeking footing on the steep decline, and when she saw Hubert waving, calling out some excited message, Ester's hopes began to stir anew.

But there was still no sign of Edmund.

She climbed to a nearby hillock, a jutting, flat-topped outcropping of blue stone.

❋ ❋ ❋

As long as he lived, Edmund would remember that moment as the only time he had been truly frightened during those challenging hours. He was lagging behind Hubert and their captive, burdened by Conrad's sword as well as his own.

It was the only instant that hope left him, as he looked around and saw all of his friends.

But no sign of Ester.

He set Conrad's sword down carefully, leaning it against a lichen-spotted stone. Old stories told of a curse that lingered on a man who showed disrespect to a weapon. Even in this moment of high feeling, it was important not to cause bad luck.

Rannulf's tanned features folded into a smile, and Nigel was pounding Edmund on the back. But the young knight could not see her and did not dare speak her name.

Until she swept down from her stony outlook.

And into his arms.

Conrad of Saxe accepted a slice of smoked ham and a rock-hard knob of cheese, glancing about the pilgrim camp with an ironic smile and a shrug.

If he expected to be rescued by his remaining brigands, he was disappointed. Just as the pilgrims were mounted and ready to set forth, the sound of a prayer was heard on the morning wind, and the creak and jingle of armor. A band of monks approached on horseback, accompanied by men-at-arms, many of them wearing sun-faded Crusader crosses.

The abbot was a white-haired man, rugged and easy in

the saddle for all his years, and he met the sight of Conrad with a laugh of relief. "You have caught the robber!" he cried.

Conrad leaned forward in his saddle, and refused to meet anyone's eye. Rannulf rode beside him, and put out a hand to steady him—or remind him where he belonged.

There was much sharing of wine sacks, and friendly exchanges, and word of how King Richard was faring, Jerusalem as yet unrescued from the Infidel. The monks called out blessings and thanksgiving as they passed, and Nigel sang out best wishes. For the first time, Ester began to believe that perhaps the fighting she had seen—and taken part in—had been good and necessary after all.

Conrad must have known the custom: A man taken hostage was expected to accept his lot with a degree of grace. His arms were unbound—personal honor, and the fear of a lance in his back, were usually enough to keep a hostage captive. But more than once that day, Rannulf had to make a hiss of warning, reaching in and taking Conrad's reins.

"Ride easy, lad," the veteran knight would say, laying a javelin across the pommel of the prisoner's saddle.

Conrad would give a nod, or turn away with a posture of hurt dignity.

More than once Ester caught the young felon's glance.

Help me, he seemed to be begging.

Please set me free.

37

THE PILGRIMS LEFT THE SNOW-MANTLED
mountains behind.

Edmund and his friends breathed the perfume of rain-rich fields and fermenting fodder, the fertile earth populated with oxen and mules, farmers and flocks of geese. It was an earthy paradise of green land and orchards, crows jeering and chattering in the pear trees, churches lifting bell towers into the forgiving sunlight.

The highway was supplied with vine-shrouded inns featuring fat roasting hens and red wine. Sir Nigel had estimated that the route from the foothills to the great city of Rome would take a fortnight, but the horses were frisky, feeding now on rich hay and freshly scythed field grass.

Conrad either knew little Frankish—the international tongue of fighting men—or he felt that the effort to speak was too much trouble. But the prisoner did have a talent that entertained his captors: He could whistle tunes. Ester recognized the holy *"Jesu Corona Virginum,"* and without blushing she admitted to herself that she recognized the ribald "My Gander's Trapped in Your Pantry."

Conrad smiled with the rest of them when Hubert capered beside a stream, and he offered Edmund a hand when the tall young knight slipped on a mossy rock. Rannulf was ever-watchful, but their captive showed no further sign of wanting to escape.

The pilgrim party left their noble hostage with a fellow countryman in Turin. Duke Conrad of Gam—the Saxon nation was replete with Conrads—was willing to part with a purse of gold marks in exchange for the blond young brigand.

"If his family wants him back," said Nigel, "they'll pay for him in turn."

The highwayman was far from strong by then. The wound Edmund had given him was festering, and he limped badly when they bid him farewell. Nigel murmured that the chances were even whether the young aristocrat lived or died.

"But I've met worse young criminals," the veteran knight allowed as they journeyed south. "And seen them flower, at length, into something fine."

Ester noted that Hubert and Edmund took no pleasure in the weight of the purse. "Better you should catch a song," said Edmund. "A tune, and maybe a soul to go with it, and carry that in a catskin bag."

But the band did not remain melancholy for many hours.

The pilgrims journeyed with increasing speed as the road reached down, through the steep passes, and close to a rocky shore. Carts laden with grapes creaked heavily along the route, and farmers greeted them cheerfully. In lands too-long bereft of honorable knights, the return of Crusaders promised fewer felons.

Homebound Crusader knights were numerous on the Italian roads, exhausted in their faded cross-splashed surcoats, most men journeying north as the pilgrims made their way south. The tidings from the Holy Land were that King Richard still failed to capture Jerusalem, and he was rumored to be about to depart and begin his journey back to his kingdom.

And there were accounts of troubles in Rome, the Orsino family all the more powerful, and King Richard's envoy Sir Maurice a virtual hostage in his own well-fortified house.

"And how fares the Lady Galena?" Hubert would ask, his voice high-pitched with anxiety.

"The good Lady Galena is well, by all accounts," said one Sir Joldwin of Exeter, a sunburned and whiskery campaigner, one midday.

"And as beautiful as new-poured cream, as I hear," he added. "But no one sets eyes on her, by night or by day. The Roman streets are safe for no one but an old crust like myself and my wizened little squire here," he laughed, indicating a sun-bronzed youth with his sword arm in a sling.

"The Romans need the taste of a few English blades," offered Sir Nigel.

"I do believe Galena's father is about to offer his own

person as hostage," said Sir Joldwin, enjoying another swallow of wine from Nigel's oft-replenished wineskin. "To secure the Lady Galena's safe passage back to England," added the knight. Such English travelers enjoyed more than one another's wine—they relished the chance to speak their mother tongue, even when the dialect and accent made conversation a challenge.

"Edmund, by my faith," said Hubert in a whisper. "We may be too late!"

"I'd avoid the Roman streets, by all that's holy," said the English knight, perhaps surprised at the intensity of the feelings in the faces around him. "Unless you're hungry for a fight."

Despite the increasing concern of the pilgrim band, the fresh peaches and warm loaves of white bread purchased along the road renewed their strength.

"We're almost there, aren't we?" Hubert began asking when they were still scores of miles from Rome.

"Only a few more days," Nigel would say.

But there was always an impediment, despite the speed with which God favored them: a herd of long-haired goats, or a charcoal burner's load, spilled across the road. Or yet another village celebrating a local saint, one unheard-of in Christendom at large—Saint Freddiano, Saint Eubaldo—processions of faithful celebrating divine help in consummating the harvest.

❄ ❄ ❄

Too late.

As they rode, their hoofbeats drummed out this message to Edmund's ears.

Each midday Nigel and Rannulf took long moments to wipe their swords with rags, and brush their cloaks and surcoats, urging every fighting man to look to his equipment, down to Clydog's eager assistants, Hervey and Eadwin, who were supplied with hatchets. Rannulf took experimental swings with his sword, cutting autumn-ruddy leaves from a beech or linden tree, nodding with satisfaction at the result.

Edmund had long noted the husbandry with which Rannulf and Nigel repaired the frayed sleeve and polished the brass hasp, and had admired this deliberate readiness—until now. Horses were curried, their shoes inspected, each mount fed just-purchased apples and buckets of fresh oats. But this detailed preparation exasperated Edmund, and Hubert, too, paced back and forth.

"Haste cheats wisdom," said Nigel, aware of Edmund's impatient refusal to paint wood tar over Surefoot's hooves. "Take every care, as always, Edmund," advised the veteran knight.

"We'll show the Romans how to bleed," piped Wowen, busy filing the roughness from a palfrey's hoof.

"No doubt," said Edmund. But would it be our blood? Edmund could not bring himself to add.

Or the blood of our enemies?

✳ ✳ ✳

Ester was fully aware of the tense anticipation of her companion knights, and she could see, as they did, the distant figures observing them, watching and spurring their mounts toward Rome.

"What will we do," asked Ida, "if the Roman gatemen don't let us in?"

One moment the band of pilgrims progressed southward, their horses increasingly well fed and strong on their splendid diet.

The next moment they fell silent.

Ester rode forward a few paces.

The holy city of Rome rose before them, brick brown and spired in the early afternoon sun. The morning cooking fires had been banked, and smoke had drifted down over the walls and towers, giving the city the semblance of a place about to become invisible.

She had dreamed so long of seeing the great city that she had to kneel before this sight, slipping down from her mount and offering tearful gratitude to God.

They continued onward, Edmund pointing out landmarks to Ester as they rode, passing the convent of Saint Agnes, down the tree-lined Via Nomentana toward the great barrier, the Porta Pia.

As they approached, the city gates opened—tall, handsome barriers—and a mounted guard rode forth under fluttering flags.

"It's an Orsino fighting force," explained Edmund. "Notice their handsome yellow sleeves. A dozen men coming out to make us welcome, Tomasso Orsino riding with them."

The Orsino scion was a much-admired swordsman in his own right. The last time Edmund had encountered the man, he was being held hostage by Sir Maurice, and the young aristocrat had proved an amiable, courteous prisoner. The sight of the colorfully outfitted Tomasso made Edmund wonder what other unexpected changes had taken place in the ancient city.

Rome had been a stew of warring families—the Orsino, Nero, and Colonna clans battling for power within the walled city. The threat to the English envoy, Sir Maurice, and his daughter, Galena, had been unyielding. Now Edmund dreaded that he and his companions might be too late.

Tomasso raised a hand in greeting, and Edmund waved back—it was hard not to like the Roman nobleman. Tomasso wore pale leather gauntlets, striking to behold, and held his horse back from the lead, not as a man reluctant to fight, but as a man of wealth who could pay others to do the sweating.

Edmund turned in his saddle to ask Nigel, "Who is that knight with the scarlet *jamb* on his shield?"

The *jamb* was a symbol of violence used very rarely as a device on banners and equipment—a severed claw. Heraldic symbols in general were only now becoming popular among knights, and most men who used a device preferred a leopard, or bird, or the ever-popular holy cross.

"I know the knight," said Rannulf, leaning to one side to spit carefully into the dust.

"Who is he, Rannulf?" asked Ester when the knight said nothing further.

"My lady," responded the master knight, "I will not soil your hearing with his name."

"He killed the entire bailey guard in that battle in Portiers some ten years ago," said Nigel. "Twelve armed men—there's a song about it. He killed a bull with one blow of a dagger, winning an emerald from the Duchess of Urle. They say no weapon can slay him."

"What is he called, this breathing legend?" asked Ester.

Nigel gave a polite smile but would not say the knight's name.

"I can kill him this moment," said Rannulf. "I am not fit for a joust, or a blade-to-blade fight—"

Ester said, "I will need my crossbow."

"I can cut out his throat," said Rannulf, "in a wink."

But even as he spoke, he saw the inappropriateness of such a murder, how it would deliver little honor—and perhaps displease Heaven.

Ester held out her hand, and Clydog brought her weapon, cradling it, lifting it with a cautionary "I sharpened the bolt just yesterday, my lady."

38

"OTHON DE BALFLEUR APPROACHES WITH his greetings," called out the muscular squire, his freshly brushed livery sporting the severed-claw insignia.

Wowen Wight took a drink of watered wine, straightened his sword belt, and sang out, "Pilgrims from the court of King Richard and Prince John respond with their finest well wishes."

Othon himself rode forward.

"My ladies, good day to you," said the knight.

He was a broad-shouldered man in leather riding armor. His hair was so close-cropped as to be little more than stubble, but he was strikingly well-formed, Ester thought, his features marred only by a pock the size of an olive where a missile must have struck his forehead some time ago.

"Othon, I heard that you were locked up in chains somewhere," said Nigel with an air of cheerful challenge.

"The man does not live who can draw a blade against Othon de Balfleur," said the squire, like a man reciting an oft-told verse, "and survive to tell the story."

"Else why did you not travel to the Holy Land?" Nigel was asking with a careless formality.

Othon made a gesture toward his forehead with his gloved hand.

"A javelin thrust by a castle guard in Aix struck my lord Othon," sang out the squire, continuing to speak on behalf of his master, "and my lord cut his head from his shoulders."

Othon and Nigel both smiled at the pithy bluntness of this report.

"It's true," said Othon, silencing his herald with a gesture. "My body was little injured, but it was dispiriting. I had to eat ox liver and drink red wine, here in Rome, until I was in good humor again." A famous, ancient hospital on the Isola Tiberina was the hospital of choice for people who could afford its care.

"But you are hale once more," said Nigel.

"By the grace of Our Lady," sang out the squire, "my lord is the most skilled fighter under Heaven. No man alive can take his life."

"I am here to keep you from entering Rome," said Othon simply. "The Orsino family has taken me into their service."

Healthy and well-armed, with a band of hirelings fingering the pommels of their swords, he would be a sore test for the pilgrims on their weary mounts.

Ester urged her horse forward a few paces.

Othon's squire took a breath to make a further

announcement, but the knight silenced him with a glance.

Othon eyed the primed crossbow, hanging by a strap from the pommel of Ester's saddle.

He inclined his body courteously from his own saddle, and said, "England has sent us a lady more lovely than the hayward's rose."

This was poor talk—any miller could have spoken as well. Ester guessed at a certain hesitation in Othon's manner. He did not know who Ester was, and was not sure what propriety might require him to do.

This was the sort of knight Ester had always mistrusted—vain and violent. She could smell the calves-foot oil that made his leather gleam. The metal fittings of his sword scabbard had been polished to a sullen luster, and the brass spikes on his gloves were bright. Ester silently asked the saints above to bless her speech.

"You will allow my queen's ladies," said Ester, "and their fellow pilgrims, into this holy city."

Othon's eyes shifted to Ida, and back to Ester. "Your queen, my lady?"

"By Heaven's mercy," said Ester evenly, "my companion and I represent Eleanor of Aquitaine, once queen of France, by God's grace queen of England and mother to—"

"Ah," said the knight. *You have said enough.*

Othon lifted his chin, giving her a challenging smile. He looked right into her eyes, a show of genial insolence. But she had noticed this trait in certain rough men before—the presence of other men quickened no fear in them, but a woman was not so easy. Besides, he sat unsteadily in the saddle for such a seasoned knight, his horse tossing and fidgeting, tonguing the bit.

The knight dismounted well, with no help from his herald, and made a show of kneeling.

"None of my men will hinder you, good lady," said Othon, rising. "But I look forward to meeting you and your fighting knights again."

He added, "Soon—on the field where blood freshens the flowers."

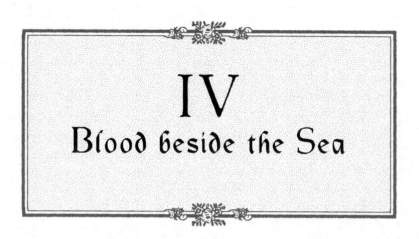

IV
Blood beside the Sea

39

EDMUND RODE HARD THROUGH THE ROMAN
streets.

Hubert urged his mount beside him, hoofbeats echoing,
a beggar scrambling out of the way, a wood seller bent
under his load hurrying across the street. Edmund was lost
for an instant, Surefoot snorting eagerly, as so many memories struck the knight—the fountains and piazzas, the
street where months before a host of Orsino pikemen had
nearly captured Galena, the churches and byways familiar
once again.

The two younger knights took the lead, all the rest following, and splashed a wide puddle entering the street
where Galena and her father lived. Just outside the envoy's
imposing dwelling they reined hard as a small army of
Orsino footmen in caps and glowing yellow sleeves confronted them. Horses bridled and pikemen jostled together.

Sir Maurice, himself on horseback, had been taken hostage, and was surrounded by a guard of silk-garbed *bravi*.
The gray-haired English banneret broke into a smile, and
called out, "I am given over to these armed men, as you see."

"Tell your hosts," said Edmund, sounding in his own ear very much the seasoned knight, "that their hospitality will not be required."

Strong joy made the noble envoy's speech falter. "Your arrival," he added, when he could speak, "is a great blessing."

The impasse was more tense than potentially violent, Edmund believed. A brace of huge dogs were held in check by an Orsino handler, and more dogs were restrained by leashes in shadowy archways.

Edmund was relieved, now, that he and the other knights had taken such care with their garments and equipment. The bright red leopard insignia on their chests, their highly polished belts and buckles, all caught the late afternoon light. The footmen took in the sight of sword and spur, and took several collective steps backward.

Ester was close behind, her mount wide-eyed at the sudden tangle of pike shafts, startled humans, and gigantic, baying dogs. She cradled her crossbow, and eased her horse to one side of the street as Rannulf, Nigel, and all the rest joined them.

"My lord," Edmund inquired of Sir Maurice, "have they hurt you or your daughter in any way?"

"No, good Edmund," said Sir Maurice, with a gentle laugh. "But by my faith, I am pleased to see every one of you."

Only one of the pikemen responded violently for the moment—Surefoot trod on the young man's foot, causing the pikeman to stagger back, into Ester's mount. The young woman had been raising her crossbow and taking aim at nothing in particular, with an air of courtly menace.

Ester's horse gave a shudder as the pikeman's weapon slipped, cutting her mount. It was not a serious wound, across the haunch of the startled animal, but at the sound of an animal in pain, the largest of the dogs slipped its leash and rushed at Edmund's horse.

Ester lifted her weapon and fired a bolt through the dog.

40

JUST AS THE DOG FELL DEAD, HOUSEHOLD
servants poured from the envoy's dwelling, men and
women, young and old, armed with clubs and stones,
kitchen cleavers and mallets. Sir Maurice gave the stentorian
commands of an experienced campaigner, and the street
rang with the sound of Orsino pikes and spears thrown
down in haste.

As long as he lived, it was not the scattered, panicked
flight of the pikemen that Edmund would remember with
magical clarity. His memory would not linger over the
image of the dead wolfhound sprawling in the muddy,
trampled street. Or the way Ester's horse tossed and pawed,
unnerved at the sight of fresh death.

He would treasure the picture of Hubert, holding
Galena by one hand and leaping—the two of them bounding—dancing in the afternoon sunlight.

Their happiness was perfect all through the banquet, goose
stuffed with duckling, and spiced tripe pie.

Sir Maurice had much to tell. Their Orsino hostage Tomasso had been exchanged for the food and wine they had been enjoying these many months, and a good quantity of gold into the bargain, and yet skirmishes and assaults on servants had been common.

Tomasso's personal retinue was stronger than ever, and the noble scion's power had increased. Even now, safe and happy as they were, Sir Maurice's walls were surrounded by Tomasso's footmen. "He's a young man of honor," said Sir Maurice. "But like many men of wealth, he finds matters of life and death little more than rough sport."

That very day Sir Maurice had at last offered himself as hostage, to ensure his daughter's safe passage home to England. "Tomasso would see that I was well wined," said the banneret, "and plied with conversation. I would have been a caged falcon, but happy enough."

Maurice had much to learn, too—about Prince John's growing power, and the way Queen Eleanor kept him carefully in check. And Sir Maurice gave a heavy sigh when he learned of Sir Jean's *routiers*, and the big knight's death.

"Prince John, I believe, will not be pleased to see all of you back again," said Sir Maurice with a rueful smile.

"He will do us no more harm," insisted Nigel. "We're the king's men, and Queen Eleanor's, too, and John for all his bad blood will not dare kill us on English soil—especially if we return with you, Sir Maurice, with your honors and good name."

Sir Maurice gave a warmhearted laugh. "You understand the royal brothers and their mother well," said the banneret. "I do believe, Sir Nigel, that Heaven may grant you a future as a man of sound advice."

Sir Nigel gave a pleased smile, but said, "I'll be grateful simply to see English rain again, and a side of English mutton."

"As Heaven wills it," responded Maurice. "But first let us find out how much the Orsino family will demand for our safe passage out of Rome."

When the yellow-sleeved messenger arrived, Edmund felt the evening sour.

Sir Maurice heard the message and shook his head.

"The Orsino family," announced Sir Maurice to his guests, "will give us safe conduct out of the city providing we pay them one thousand gold marks."

The price was absurdly, brutally high. Conrad of Saxe himself had been worth only fifty marks—and that from the purse of a fellow Saxon.

"We will fight our way out," said Rannulf.

"I do believe you will find," said Sir Maurice, "that once you are here, it is not so easy to escape."

"What alternative do they propose?" asked Edmund.

"A battle between champions," said Sir Maurice.

The gathering fell silent.

"Our single best fighter," Sir Maurice continued, "against their champion Othon de—what is he called?"

Edmund stood.

Nigel buried his face in his hands, and Rannulf gave a great sigh.

"With God as my witness—" began Edmund.

"Sit down, dear Edmund," said Nigel gently.

"Who else should do the fighting, Sir Nigel?" protested Edmund. "Heaven has forestalled Rannulf's healing, and I'll not suffer Hubert to risk his life for mine again."

The great house of the banneret Sir Maurice was a warren of halls and side rooms, and Ester had to search to find Edmund.

She discovered him at last, sitting with Hubert in the armorer's chambers, surrounded by samples of fighting gloves. Spiked gauntlets and supple riding gloves, full-sleeved iron chain mail and iron-braced grips. The items of apparel looked so much like severed hands that she hesitated for a moment to enter the room.

"Dog skin, bull hide, or a chain-mail mitten," said Edmund with a laugh. "Which would you prefer, my lady?"

"Or this?" said Hubert, holding up a gauntlet of scale work, an armored grip so heavily metalled it clanked as the knight shook it.

"I have a sacred thing," she said. She corrected herself, saying, "A holy object. A relic that may help us all."

Much later that night there was a tap on the brass-hinged door to Sir Maurice's chamber.

Sir Nigel and Sir Rannulf were at a table with Sir

Maurice, and although each man had a silver cup of wine, no one was drinking.

A servant murmured in Sir Maurice's ear, and the envoy gave a nod.

"I have seen how such jousts can conclude, gentlemen," said Ester when she had joined the three veteran knights, Edmund beside her. "There will be fighting as the crowd joins in, and none of us will ever see our homes again."

The three knights were standing, showing respect to the young lady, but each wore an expression of anxious doubt.

"You may be right, Lady Ester," said Nigel.

"Only a holy sign," said the young woman, "or a sacred relic will move such a crowd to peace."

"Good Ester, I have seen a Roman crowd," said Sir Maurice, "in drunken riot on Easter Day."

"Gentle knights," said Ester, "see what Queen Eleanor gave me to protect all of us from harm."

She held out her hand.

An oblong frame depicted the image of Saint George slaying the twisting dragon. The monster's tail wound all the way around the inset rock crystal, and within the transparent stone a bright, thorn-shaped object gleamed in radiant colors as the candlelight played upon it.

"I have heard the queen had such a noble relic," breathed Nigel, "and kept it well-hidden."

"What is it?" asked Rannulf.

"My father says it is a shard of opal-stone, and nothing

more," said Ester. "But some say it is the claw of the dragon, slain by Saint George."

"Is it indeed?" asked Sir Maurice. He did not reach out to touch it—even a man of fine-spun common sense was impressed by such relics.

Only Rannulf would take it from Ester's hand. Dragons, griffins, narwhals, and other such creatures were little understood. If Rannulf were confronted with one, he imagined that he would find it no more fearful than many humans.

"There is a pebble of bone in here, as well," said the veteran knight.

"It is from the fighting hand," said Ester, "of the dragon-slayer."

Rannulf met her gaze wonderingly. He set the reliquary down firmly on the table, and took a step back. He knelt, joined by his fellow knights, including Sir Maurice, as though the fighting saint himself had entered the room.

"You received this from Queen Eleanor, Lady Ester?" inquired Sir Maurice when he was on his feet again.

"Indeed I did, Sir Maurice," said Ester. "And I believe that this holy relic can win us passage back home to my father and my lady queen."

The other men were still kneeling prayerfully, even as Sir Maurice poured a cup of wine and offered it to Ester.

"God help us," said Sir Maurice, speaking as though to the shivering candlelight. "We may just possibly see England again."

41

ROME WAS EVERY BIT THE CITY OF HOLY
wonders, as Ester had dreamed.

Accompanied by Edmund and squire Wowen, along
with a band of well-armed servants, she prayed at the
Church of Santa Sabina, thanking Heaven for the recovered health of her father, and asking for the repose of her
mother's soul. She joyed at the sight of the Colosseum,
where Christian martyrs had been killed under the pagan
emperors of ancient times, and she marveled at the great
castle of Saint Michael across the Tiber River, a citadel
greater in girth and height than the Tower of London.

But she could not help noticing the haughty eyes of the
Orsino hirelings, and the sauntering manner of such men as
they called to one another down the long, shadowy streets.
And the guarded, exasperated glances of fruit sellers and
fishmongers, and the fact that if an Orsino servant stole a
smoked eel from a basket, no one joined the fish seller's
wife in chasing the laughing youth.

Many windows in Rome remained heavily shuttered,
bolted against trouble.

Galena proved a worthy companion, gentle of voice and manner, and quick to point out the easiest way back home—and the safest. No man or woman of note went out without a band of armed men.

This gave Rome the quality of being always on parade, the oil-cured armor and *tink-a-chink* of chain mail adding a festive air to the morning market. But the holy city was plainly a town ready for trouble, too many men testing the edge of their battle-axes against their gloved thumbs. Galena pointed out the kingfisher-blue livery of the Nero family, and the jaunty scarlet of the Colonna servants, and Ester had seen enough of life to recognize unhappiness in the smiles of the men and women of Rome, waiting for this era of Orsino insolence to pass.

Ester tried to believe that her own peaceful interlude would stretch on forever, warm autumn afternoons beside the rosemary and the late-season roses on Sir Maurice's roof garden. Edmund was so often eager to tell her about some new wonder he had seen—an albino goat, or a Nubian giant from the Nile. One afternoon he brought her the soft fur of an unborn lamb, traded by caravans, he reported excitedly, all the way from Persia.

It was his enthusiasm she loved more than anything else, his excitement at the sight of a jackdaw chasing a hawk from a church tower, his smile when a wine seller broke into song. She tried to promise herself she would never spend a day away from the sturdy knight, as though she did not know all the while the great danger he was soon to face.

But it was only a week, no longer, while the preparations were made, a site chosen on the beach near the old port of Ostia—even Orsino wishes could not offset the church's edict against jousts within a city's walls.

Ester and Ida stitched, their silk-shot needles kissing their thimbles, working by daylight, and by the oil lamps of evening. They were preparing their sacred banner, and they intended it to dazzle.

And to surprise.

Galena and her servants brought them bolts of silk, green and scarlet, rare and expensive cloth that whispered as the shears cut it through.

Ester drew a pattern with a wedge of wax, outlining the shapes. She sewed with haste, but never had her needle done such cunning work.

It look long hours.

"I do get right weary," said Ida. Then, at a glance from Ester, she sat up straight and blinked. "But not too weary, by my faith."

One evening Wowen Wight was dressed in the leopard-emblem livery of King Richard and recited his announcement, practicing as Ester and Edmund and all the rest looked on.

Wowen's accents were those of Nottingham, but his words were the universal courtly Frankish of couriers and knights, the language spoken, in one form or another, from Paris to Sicily, wherever ballads were sung and swords drawn.

"Responding to the Orsino challenge, Edmund Strongarm, by the grace of God, Crusader and knight of King Richard and Prince John—" Wowen stopped.

"What's wrong, Wowen?" asked Edmund.

The young squire replied, "Those words will never sound like music, my lords."

"It sounds entirely proper," said Nigel. "Prince John raised good Edmund to knighthood, after all."

"My lords," protested Wowen, "why mention the prince?"

"Go, then, and say it however you will," said Edmund. "But tell Othon de Balfleur to be at the water's edge by noon."

42

EDMUND WAS FIRMLY PERCHED ON HIS
spirited new horse, a heavy fighting mount called Pigmeo—
"Pygmy."

This was an ironic name, since the stallion was heavy,
big-headed, and the young knight felt dangerously far from
the ground. Travel-worn Surefoot was stabled safely, eating
sweet grass and getting fat. Edmund missed him now.

Pigmeo tossed his massive head as Rannulf seized the
bridle. The horse quieted for an instant at the seasoned
knight's touch.

Edmund had decided to fight without gloves, bare-
handed, following Rannulf's advice. The weathered knight
reassured Edmund now, "You'll grip the sword the better
for it, Edmund."

Rannulf believed that Edmund was still green as a
swordsman, but as strong as any fighter the veteran had
ever seen. Some artful word or blessing was in order, but
Rannulf knew only life and its opposite.

"Edmund, if Othon hurts you—" began Rannulf.

Slays you, he meant, but it was best not to put a fear into words. "If he unseams you in the least—" Strong feeling broke his voice.

On the landward side of the jousting site, folk were still arriving, sellers of smoked fish and hot, highly seasoned pies calling their wares. The entire city of Rome seemed to have come out to the seashore, crowding the long sloping beach not far from the mouth of the river Tiber. And they came ready for trouble, draymen and bakers armed with cudgels, scarlet-clad Colonna sympathizers with swords at their belts. The Nero faction was well-represented, too, outfitted in blue and bristling with dirks, daggers, and broadswords, each family ready to skirmish if the day's fight boiled over into a melee.

Tomasso Orsino sat under a bright blue canopy. The nobleman would be the final arbiter of the day's events. If Tomasso felt satisfied that honor had been fulfilled, Edmund and his companions would be free to embark. As Edmund caught his eye, the yellow-mantled aristocrat gave a handsome smile, and lifted a hand bejeweled with an amber ring.

Edmund gave a bow and worked hard to force every fear from his heart. A tantalizing presence, the great vessel *Santa Monica* rolled with the soft swells offshore. The ship was due to sail as soon as the joust was finished—if Edmund was victorious. If the saints—and Tomasso Orsino—willed it, day's end would see Edmund and his companions happily stowed on this prosperous ship. Boats along the waterline were guarded by men Sir Maurice had paid well, and the way to safety was so close that Edmund felt the cruelty of his own hopefulness.

He thrust the thought of a well-provisioned, short sea voyage with Ester by his side entirely out of his mind. Edmund wanted to pray yet again, and he wanted to press his lips against Ester's once more.

And he wished he could express his gratitude to Nigel and Rannulf, and vanquish the look of intense concern in the eyes of the two experienced knights. He raised a hand to Hubert, who watched white-faced from a distance, putting on a brave smile. Galena and Sir Maurice looked on nearby, anxiously hopeful that they would be able to leave Italian soil.

Blessed by Holy Communion, his knees still sandy from having knelt before the priest, Edmund wanted to sing out that if he died today, he bore no malice toward any man. It was proper to say such a thing before legal combat, but Othon was in haste, already hefting the jousting lance, helmeted and waving his squire away, well before the crowd had fully arrived.

Noon was barely upon them. *Too quick*, Edmund wanted to protest.

There should have been more ceremony, more time while the banner of Saint George that Ester and Ida had made could be brought to the fore of the crowd. It was nowhere to be seen yet, although Edmund had heard it described—a silk standard topped by the sacred relic, firmly fastened with wrought gold wire.

Surely Ester would not be late. Indeed, she was not late at all—it was Othon who was too early, waving his servants back as he raced his horse back and forth, splashing salt foam.

Edmund wanted to call out before the world, "I die with peace in my heart."

But Edmund ran through his mind the names of lively folk who had died in recent seasons. Otto, Edmund's former master, a good-hearted moneyer but none too honest. Osbert the servant, whose loyalty and desire to serve were matched by his powers as a thief. Edmund recalled the irrepressible squire Miles, with his bawdy songs, and the brave steed Winter Star, slain in the battle of Arsuf.

And the hostages from Acre, some two thousand innocent men, women, and children, put to the sword at King Richard's command.

The young knight did not want to take Sir Othon's life.

But the heavily furnished Othon had finished adjusting his armor. He sported more iron than Edmund—with high chain-mail sleeves attached to his spiked gauntlets, and uncommon plate armor protecting his front and back.

No wonder he was such a man killer, Edmund thought, if he started lancing his opponents while their helmets were barely set. Edmund felt the wisdom of Rannulf's advice— too much armor weighed a fighter down and made him a slower target. Still, he felt that he could have worn another layer of quilt under his helmet, or doubled up the chain mail under his surcoat. "Youth and strength will be your advantage," Rannulf had asserted.

Othon rocked into his charge. For the moment Pigmeo was much more eager to fight than Edmund. It was not the first time the young knight had marveled that so many horses loved combat. Edmund did not need to urge the heavy mount forward. Pigmeo plunged, grunting with effort and enthusiasm as Othon's plumed helmet grew closer. The big knight was upon Edmund, clods of sandy beach flying—and then he was past, neither man making contact with the other.

The crowd thundered.

Edmund was not encouraged—far from it. Othon was an experienced lancer, while the youthful knight was anything but a master with the weapon. Indeed, Othon's lance had whistled past, not missing by more than a hand's span, while Edmund had made only an awkward flourish with his own shaft.

Again, from the new direction, Othon coursed down the beach toward Edmund, but this time the young knight was ready, his lance properly couched—nestled under his arm, the shaft steady. But then the sharp point dipped, as though compelled by its own will, the long, dangerous weapon aiming ever downward as Pigmeo rocked into a gallop. The lance fell even lower, and at last the point stabbed hard into the sandy beach.

The force levered Edmund, and sent him flying from

his saddle, over Pigmeo's head. The lance broke into pieces, and Edmund rolled, helmeted and padded under his chain mail, and unhurt.

Unhurt, but as he climbed to his feet, unsteady.

And not completely unhurt, after all—the wind had been knocked from his body, every bit of air, and he could not breathe.

43

AT LAST, EDMUND COULD DRAW A STEADY breath again, just as Wowen and Hubert were running with a new lance, a long pale weapon. Edmund motioned to his friends, *Hurry!*

But again it was too late.

Othon was on the attack, before the lance could arrive, even as Edmund stood flat-footed. Wowen and Hubert scattered. Edmund had little time to form a plan. He took a step to one side, so the lance passed over his shoulder, and seized the horse's bridle.

Edmund turned the charger's head, hauling with all his strength. The steed was pulled out of its course by his effort, and with his other hand Edmund found the flowing trapper—the cloth that hung down from the saddle.

Edmund called out—as drivers of dray horses did on market morning in Nottingham—a long syllable, half song, half warning. The sound from within his helmet was both magnified and distorted, and Othon's mount was startled for an instant—just as Edmund had hoped it would be. And Othon was an impatient horseman, sawing heavily at the reins, failing to lean away from Edmund's weight.

The big knight tried to strike Edmund's helmet with a brass-spiked fist, swayed in the saddle, and fell off just as his horse stumbled and went down.

Edmund drew his sword as his opponent lumbered to his feet. Othon was not long in pulling his own blade from its sheath, but then the crowd—which had been calling and jeering, crying out and encouraging in several languages—began to fall silent.

Ester rode a palfrey, with the banner held high, the image of Saint George in deep red and blue, fastened against a green background.

The sacred relics caught the light, the dragon's claw and the blessed remnant of King Richard's patron saint held high for the gathered folk to behold. The claw of the dragon gleamed, and the single, fleshless finger bone of the saint was like wrought gold in the sunlight.

If Othon saw any of this, he gave no sign at first. He cut at Edmund, just missing, and cut again, as the young knight found firmer footing in the sand.

Many in the crowd were kneeling, and soon the mass of men and women looked on rapt, no mouth lifting a call, no hand reaching for a weapon. By then Othon could not continue to ignore the sweeping hush.

The knight half turned to take in the spectacle, sunlight gleaming off the iridescent claw of the dragon and the gold-bright relic of the saint.

Othon did not move, caught by the vision.

The two horses found each other and fought, grunting, foam flying. But Pigmeo was the better fighter, forcing Othon's shaken horse backward.

Othon hefted his sword again. Edmund began his own assault, hacking efficiently at Othon as the legendary knight stirred once more to combat. Let me not kill him, prayed Edmund.

Too much killing.

No more.

The riderless horses continued to fight nearby. Edmund struck Othon well. The young knight's strokes nearly drove the weapon from the older man's grasp. His sword whistling through the air, Edmund continued the attack, and struck his adversary's helmet so hard the iron gave off a spark. Othon fell to his knees.

Panicked, Othon's horse was kicking out at nothing. Edmund saw what was about to happen, but could not make a move to stop it. The horse's rear hoof struck Othon's helmet as the knight knelt motionless. With an ugly sound, like an iron bell sundered, the armor cracked.

Othon sprawled on the sand.

44

EDMUND HAD TO WAIT WHILE HUBERT
and Wowen dragged the two ill-tempered horses away, and
then Edmund hauled at his opponent's fractured helmet.
The young knight tugged hard, and found himself gazing
down at the dazed and blinking eyes of his enemy.

Yield he could not say. Or perhaps he did say the word,
the syllable resounding in his helmet.

Othon reached, but his sword was far off, half-buried in
sand.

Yield, or you will bleed, Edmund tried to say again.

Othon reached again, groped, and seized his weapon.

Did Edmund say the words, or only hear them in his
soul? *Please do not force me to kill you.*

Othon rolled, and struggled to one knee. Then he held
his sword out, hilt-foremost.

And Edmund took it.

The crowd rejoiced as Edmund held up the two swords,
the steel cold and heavy in his hands.

He did not see what happened next, as he settled the two swords respectfully on the sand—but he sensed the crowd's intaken breath. He caught a glimpse of Othon's shadow, shifting, lunging, as the older knight drew a glinting span from his mail sleeve and thrust it at Edmund.

Edmund's instant thought was that the stunned Othon was holding out a cross, or some other blessed object, and giving it to the victor as a further token of surrender. The young knight stepped toward his vanquished opponent, in a helpful spirit, only to see the white gleam of a dagger.

Bare-handed as he was, Edmund struggled to get a grip on the brass-spiked gloves and mail-clad limbs of the older knight. Edmund sensed that as rapt as the crowd had been, all calm would be lost, and a violent melee follow, if the fight did not end with a definite outcome, and at once.

The dagger scraped the hardened iron of Edmund's helmet, the blade working hard, sawing at the chain mail protecting the young knight's neck, seeking flesh.

Edmund wrenched the man's arm, gripping it and twisting, throwing the big knight down and feeling the bones give within their iron-mesh armor. Bones snapped. Edmund seized the dagger and felt its handle warm in his grasp, a fine steel blade.

Kill him, said a voice in his soul.

Cut his throat—it is what he deserves.

Edmund wanted to take Othon's life at that moment. He desired it as much as he had ever wanted meat and drink.

✳ ✳ ✳

But he hurled the weapon.

It spun end over end, gleaming. The blade plunged far off, into the sea, over the heads of the pikemen guarding the boats, nearly all the way to the peaceful bulk of the *Santa Monica*.

The crowd was silent—perhaps dazzled by events, Edmund thought, or stunned by lost wagers, or expectant that Othon would rise again to some new treachery.

Othon did indeed try to rise for a long moment, but his injured arm kept him where he was, as though the broken limb had taken root in the sand, leaving the knight kicking helplessly.

And then the crowd's silence broke. A tumult of cheering and song deafened Edmund as he waited for some further sign to tell him that the contest was complete and the day won.

The knight was uncertain even then, unwilling to give himself over to joy. Tomasso Orsino was making his way across the sand, the crowd roaring, and Edmund tried to read the gaze of this Roman nobleman.

Tomasso grew close, and Edmund braced himself, unsure what the aristocrat intended to do.

Edmund said, "I wish to go home with my companions."

Tomasso made a show of not understanding.

"With God's blessing, and your kind permission, noble Tomasso," said the knight, in careful Frankish, "we will leave today for England."

Tomasso laughed quietly, as though moved to pure, easy friendliness by the day's events.

Edmund gathered his will, and was about to speak again, when Tomasso's smile and quiet laugh silenced him.

"Depart, then, Edmund Strongarm," the nobleman said. "As the blessed Saint George wills it—you may go home."

As Edmund took Ester into his arms, he heard Nigel's voice calling, "To England!"

To England.